Gathering
Sparks

Gathering Sparks

Interviews from *PARABOLA MAGAZINE*

Selected by David Appelbaum and Joseph Kulin

PARABOLA BOOKS
NEW YORK

PUBLISHED BY
PARABOLA BOOKS
656 Broadway
New York, NY 10012
WEBSITE: www.parabola.org

The paper used in this publication meets the minimum
requirements of the American National Standard for
Permanence of Paper for Printed Library Materials
Z39.48–1984

LIBRARY OF CONGRESS CATALOGING-IN-PUBLICATION DATA
Gathering sparks : interviews from Parabola magazine.— 1st ed.
   p. cm.
  ISBN 0-930407-53-9 (pbk. : alk. paper)
  1. Religion. 2. Mythology

BL50 .G34 2001
200—dc21

                           2001051020

DESIGN BY
Davidson Design, Inc., New York

PRINTED IN THE UNITED STATES OF AMERICA

ARTWORK:
PAGE 152, 154 copyright © Marvin Barrett
PAGE 153, 184 copyright © Karen Benzian
PAGE 152, 163 copyright © Brother Chuck
PAGE 108, 120 copyright © Ellen Dooling Draper
PAGES 63, 70, 108, 110, 153 [BROOK AND GYATSO], 177, 192
copyright © Lee B. Ewing
PAGE 89, 90 copyright © Frederick Franck
PAGE 109, 137 copyright © Pablo Hillman
PAGES 10, 11, 18, 27 copyright © Lorraine Kisly
PAGE 109, 132 copyright © Kanatsiohareke/Tom Porter
PAGE 89, 100 copyright © Roger Lipsey
PAGE 89, 94 copyright © Henk Pander
PAGE 10, 12 copyright © Don Purdue (WNET TV)
PAGE 152, 169 copyright © William Segal
PAGE 63, 64 copyright © Nancy Stetson
PAGE 11, 41 copyright © Alice van Buren
PAGE 109, 145 copyright © Jojo Whilden
PAGE 63, 77 copyright © Rosalie Winard

The story "Gathering Sparks" is from Gabriel's Palace:
Jewish Mystical Tales by Howard Schwartz. Copyright
© 1994 by Howard Schwartz. Used by permission of
Oxford University Press Inc. and Ellen Levine Literary
Agency, Inc.

Gathering Sparks

ONE ROSH HODESH THE ARI LED HIS DISCIPLES OUTSIDE AT NIGHT and told them to follow him. He led them without a torch, so that only the stars lighted their way. Yet it seemed to them that there was another light that guided them, an aura that emanated from the Ari.

At last they reached their destination, the tomb of Rabbi Shimon bar Yohai. There the Ari began to pray with great intensity, and all the others joined him, swaying back and forth, until it seemed as if they were being rocked in a cradle of stars.

At last they completed the prayers, and there was silence. This lasted long into the night, and for all of them it was as if they had discovered the world on the first day of creation.

Then, at midnight, the Ari began to speak. And every word seemed to them like one of the words with which the world was created. For there he revealed the mystery of the Shattering of the Vessels and the Gathering of the Sparks. How, long before the sun cast a shadow, before the Word was spoken that brought the heavens and the earth into being, a flame emerged from an unseen point. And how sparks of light sprang forth from the center of that flame, concealed in shells that set sail everywhere, above and below, like a fleet of ships, each carrying its cargo of light.

How the frail vessels broke open, split asunder, and all the sparks were scattered, like sand, like seeds, like stars.

That is when they learned why they had been created—to search for the sparks, no matter where they were hidden, and as each one was revealed, to raise it up and redeem it. For when all the scattered sparks had been gathered, the vessels would be restored, and the footsteps of the Messiah would be heard at last.

Just as the Ari finished speaking, a comet streaked across the sky. And when they saw this, all of them were filled with wonder, for they understood that they were not the only ones who had heard the words of the Ari that night. The words had also been heard in heaven.

—PALESTINE, SIXTEENTH CENTURY

Contents

8   Foreword
          MARVIN BARRETT

The Roots of Reality

12   On Waking Up
          JOSEPH CAMPBELL
          Vol. 7, No. 1, "Sleep"

18   The Only Freedom
          HELEN M. LUKE
          Vol. 11, No. 2, "Mirrors"

27   Worshipping Illusions
          MARION WOODMAN
          Vol. 12, No. 2, "Addiction"

41   Recovering a Common Language
          KATHLEEN RAINE
          Vol. 8, No. 3, "Words of Power"

48   If She's Not Gone, She Lives There Still
          P. L. TRAVERS AND MICHAEL DAMES
          Vol. 3, No. 1, "Sacred Space"

Finding Our Place

64   Belonging
          THOMAS BERRY
          Vol. 24, No. 1, "Nature"

70   The Risk of Evolution
          JOSEPH CHILTON PEARCE
          Vol. 17, No. 2, "Labyrinth"

77   The Nature of Consciousness
          OLIVER SACKS
          Vol. 22, No. 3, "Conscience and Consciousness"

Confronting Our Humanity

90   The Human Face
          FREDERICK FRANCK
          Vol. 23, No. 3, "Fear"

94   Point of Return
          URSULA K. LE GUIN
          Vol. 23, No. 1, "Millennium"

100   We Are All Witnesses
          ELIE WIESEL
          Vol. 10, No. 2, "Exile"

The Indigenous Perspective

110 If One Thing Stands, Another Will Stand Beside It
CHINUA ACHEBE
Vol. 17, No. 3, "The Oral Tradition"

120 Giveaway for the Gods
ARTHUR AMIOTTE
Vol. 15, No. 4, "Hospitality"

132 Why We're Here Today
CHIEF TOM PORTER
Vol. 24, No. 2, "Prayer & Meditation"

137 Singing the World
HEATHER VALENCIA
Vol. 25, No. 2, "Riddle & Mystery"

145 Moving Through Milestones
SOBONFU SOMÉ
Vol. 25, No. 4, "Fate and Fortune"

Approaching Presence

154 The Silent Guide
FATHER BEDE GRIFFITHS
Vol. 11, No. 1, "The Witness"

163 Awakening to the Present
FATHER THOMAS KEATING
Vol. 15, No. 1, "Time & Presence"

169 Inviting Hell into Heaven
WILLIAM SEGAL
Vol. 24, No. 2, "Prayer & Meditation"

177 Reaching for the Trapeze
PETER BROOK
Vol. 15, No. 1, "Time & Presence"

184 The Command Is to Hear
RABBI ADIN STEINSALTZ
Vol. 19, No. 1, "The Call"

192 The Experience of Change
TENZIN GYATSO (H.H. THE DALAI LAMA)
Vol. 15, No. 1 "Time & Presence"

Foreword

IN RECENT YEARS THE INTERVIEW HAS BEEN CONCERNED most conspicuously with the rich and the famous, the talented and the successful, the for-the-moment notorious. The questions posed are intended to ferret out the tragedy, the trauma, the lucky tricks or accidents that explain or explain away the celebrity we are focused upon. Sometimes, such is the nature of TV and the popular press, the interviewer is as celebrated as the interviewee. In any case the ego seems to be all in all, in a journalistic game of hide-and-seek, of gotcha! or in rare instances of appropriate, deserved approval.

There is, however, another species of interview that ignores the personal and seeks out the universal. It might be said to begin with Socrates and has threaded its way through the intervening centuries wherever the curious and venturesome, the stubborn, the dissatisfied, the truly devoted seek truth and are willing to share it. These interviews, these dialogues and colloquies have to do not with personality but with an inquiry into the meaning of life, knowledge that some generous human being is willing to pass along.

It is to this category of interview that PARABOLA Magazine has for the past quarter-century addressed itself.

IN SOME OF THE EXCHANGES THAT FOLLOW, THE TRUTH seems to be happened upon almost by accident, questioner and questioned being equally surprised and delighted.

In others, the authorities—and all of those interviewed are in one way or another possessors of a special knowledge—are allowed to speak for themselves and for the body of wisdom they represent. Sometimes they will speak with an unusual and personal eloquence, as Frederick Franck does in his consideration of "Fear," or Rabbi Steinsaltz in exploring the meaning of "The Call." In other interviews, we are introduced to a specific form of wisdom peculiar to the person questioned, as in the interviews with Chinua Achebe and Arthur Amiotte, where arcane indigenous traditions are explored and explained. A weighty exchange with Oliver Sacks on "Conscience and Consciousness" is illuminated by an underlying humor, while archaeologist Michael Dames' encounter with P. L. Travers explores the significance of sacred space as these two experts urge each other on, the reader profiting doubly thereby.

In the personality-driven interviews that prevail in the popular press, it is the sudden revelation of where the film star or politician, the writer, artist, or musician is coming from that excites the reader or viewer: the mistakes he or she has made, the lowest common denominator of his or her experience revealed, the gossip confirmed, denied, compounded. In the interviews that follow, where ideas and truth are the common concern and personalities are forgotten, the revelations are of an entirely different order. These are people who know and are willing to share their knowledge with their interrogator and us, a knowledge that cannot fail to be instructive and in many cases crucial.

For me, of all the interviews I have done as a practicing journalist for fifty years—and they have numbered in the hundreds—the most remarkable may have been that with William Segal, included in this volume. Every note I sounded as his questioner he took up and made a chord. I still shiver when I read it, as though I were there again in his apartment high above Manhattan, surrounded by a few objects of consummate beauty—a bit of Chinese calligraphy, a Tang horse, a serene antique head of the Buddha—occasionally being interrupted by the comments of his parrot Suki as he paused for thought before proceeding to the next illuminating answer.

A close second was my encounter with Father Bede Griffiths in his primitive ashram in a grove beside the holy river Cavery in south India, a world away from the British Isles where he had his first and lasting conversion. Across the clearing from his simple hut was a manger with a dozen cows chewing their cuds, nodding their heads as if in agreement with what their wise master was saying.

Two different environments, two disparate traditions drawing on the same inexhaustible store of wisdom.

What those two men told me, correcting gently the course of my questioning, setting me right, leading me to some valuable insight, it is my privilege to share with the reader. And my revelatory experiences are just two among the many in the succeeding pages.

One feels in these interviews that one is encountering just the tip of the iceberg, the epitome, the harvest of a lifetime pursuit of reality. If after reading one we wish to learn more, that is the mark of a successful interview.

For me there are no failures in this volume. There are twenty-two opened doors.

—**MARVIN BARRETT**, NEW YORK, MAY 2001

The Roots of Reality

On Waking Up

JOSEPH CAMPBELL

Vol. 7, No. 1
"Sleep"

The Only
Freedom

HELEN M. LUKE

Vol. 11, No. 2
"Mirrors"

Worshipping
Illusions

Recovering a
Common
Language

If She's Not Gone,
She Lives There Still

MARION WOODMAN

KATHLEEN RAINE

**P. L. TRAVERS AND
MICHAEL DAMES**

Vol. 12, No. 2
"Addiction"

Vol. 8, No. 3
"Words of Power"

Vol. 3, No. 1
"Sacred Space"

On Waking Up

An Interview with Joseph Campbell

From PARABOLA Vol. 7, No. 1, "Sleep"

> **Joseph Campbell** was an internationally known scholar, author, and lecturer in the field of comparative mythology. His books include **The Hero with a Thousand Faces** (Princeton University Press), **The Masks of God** (Arkana), and **The Power of Myth** with Bill Moyers (Doubleday).

PARABOLA: On the presupposition that humans are capable of higher levels of consciousness than those in which they ordinarily exist, sleep is a metaphor for what we think of as our waking state—and from which it behooves us some-how to awake. The Buddha, as we know, means The Awakened. St. Paul urged his fellow Christians, "Let us not sleep as do others, but let us watch."

It is this metaphorical aspect of sleep and awakening that I'd like to discuss.

JOSEPH CAMPBELL: One of the classic texts on sleep is the *Mandukya Upanishad*, which speaks of four stages of con-sciousness: waking consciousness, dream consciousness, deep, dreamless sleep, and then the mystery of going into deep, dreamless sleep *awake*—which is when one breaks through the plane of darkness into undifferentiated consciousness.

The way in which the metaphor of sleep and waking is used relates to exactly that state. The Awakened One, the Buddha, has awakened to that undifferentiated conscious-ness. From that point of view, we who have not waked to that are asleep in our rational, normal, and even dreaming lives. That awakening is the great breakthrough.

Another image for this sleep-state that we are in is Water. Jesus said to his apostles, "I will make you fishers of men"—pulling the normal fish-men out of the water of their sleep and bringing them to their potential fully human consciousness. This is a motif from the Orphic tradition where Orpheus is the fisher who lifts us out of our fish-state and brings us to the light at the top of the water.

P: The water standing for the unconscious state of ordinary life—"sleep."

JC: Well, what we call consciousness is part of that unconsciousness—unconsciousness of the solar light. That's the big pitch of these mythological metaphors.

P: The miracle of Jesus walking on the water in the storm comes to mind—on one level a dramatic demonstration of control over the forces of nature, but on another level symbolic of dominion over the turbulent dream world in which we are being tossed around.

JC: Yes. The Buddha walked on the water, too, five hundred years earlier. Walking on water and walking on fire are standard motifs.

P: You mentioned that the Upanishads speak of going into this deep, dreamless sleep while awake.

JC: Yes. That's the function of yoga.

P: So that one is living in both worlds at the same time.

JC: Yes. There's a saying in one of the Upanishads—something like: "We go every night to that Brahma world where the treasure is." It also says that, as one can walk over a buried treasure day after day and night after night, so do we walk over that Brahma world in our sleep without knowing it. We come that close to illumination every night, but. . . .

P: So that the adept, the sage, works to perfect the ability to stay conscious in his sleep?

JC: Oh, in fact that's one of the monastic disciplines, where you go to sleep pronouncing a mantra of waking knowledge—kind of a fishing line to carry you from waking to transcendent consciousness. But the fact that the Buddha means "the waked up" teaches the main lesson here.

P: And the role of the Buddha—or the Savior—is to wake up other people?

JC: That's right!

P: Has American Indian mythology much of this imagery of sleep and waking? Black Elk had a vision in sleep.

JC: Black Elk had a tremendous vision—a revelation through sleep of the Great Truth. He says at one point: "I saw myself on the Central Mountain of the World. The Central Mountain of the World is Harney Peak in South Dakota." Then he added: "But the Central Mountain of the World is everywhere." *That* is the word of one who has waked up! He understands the function of the cult image—the cult-focus on a specific image or idea of sanctuary. But that is not the final reference. That is but the finger pointing to the moon—the metaphor intending the Transcendent. That's something that has been lost, I would say, in the Judeo-Christian tradition. They tend to think Jerusalem is the Central Mountain of the World.

P: That's the problem of our tradition, that it's historical and linear.

JC: It's a killer, that problem! The function of symbols is to be transparent to the transcendent, and the whole character of the Judeo-Christian tradition is opaque to the transcendent. Everybody else has got the hang of it except these people going around trying to convert the world to their concretization of the idea of God, who sits there as a kind of roadblock. It's really fantastic! There's a saying in Zen Buddhism: "If you see the Buddha coming down the road, *kill him!*" As long as you're stuck with the Buddha—haven't killed him on the road—you're in devotion; you haven't got past the pairs of opposites and the cult objects to realize *Tat Twam Asi*—That Art Thou. If you have concretized the image of the transcendent, get rid of your image. Meister Eckhart tells us: "The ultimate leave-taking is the leaving of God for GOD." We're stuck with Jesus, who physically died on the cross to return in unity to the Father. But we haven't taken that passage through the Cross seriously enough.

P: The injunction to us to die in Christ isn't taken seriously either.

JC: Of course not! We think it's dying into Jesus. But Christ isn't Jesus. Christ is the eternal Second person of the Blessed Trinity—yesterday, today, and tomorrow. Jesus is an historical character. He has been identified with Christ, just as each of us ought to be. But so many people who think they're Christians have become fixed on a concrete reference. Even Yahweh is as concrete as can be. Remember, Hegel called him "the gaseous vertebrate."

P: Western religion today tends to be ethically oriented.

JC: Yes, sin and the atonement of sin. That puts a screen before us, and we can't penetrate through to the metaphysical, beyond all the pairs of opposites—good and evil, male and female, action and inaction, man and God. We're stuck with God in his Heaven and Satan in Hell—the ultimate pair of opposites! Adam and Eve were thrown out of the Garden when they ate the fruit of the knowledge of the pairs of opposites.

P: And the role of the Serpent—at least in the Gnostic tradition. . . .

JC: Is to wake you. Absolutely! The Serpent did his best to turn them away from that god who was an ethical god, a righteous god, full of vengeance. That's why the Orphic cults—the Gnostic, snake-worshipping cults—saw Jesus as the Second Coming of the Serpent. Because with Jesus, the law of Yahweh, the Old Testament, was transcended—we finally got rid of it. But then the Christians went right back. Their tradition is the Old Testament tradition all over again! Good and evil, right and wrong, sin and atonement.

P: It seems to me that the Egyptians may have known all about this.

JC: I *know* that the Egyptians knew all about this. There are enough clues in their art. And they had connections, too, with Indian ideas centuries before India had them. For example, I have a picture of that scene of the weighing of the heart against the feather that dates back to about 1400 B.C.E., in which the upright of the scale has exactly seven little swellings, corresponding to the seven *chakras*. And you know that hippopotamus-like animal that devours anyone whose heart is heavier than a feather? Well the nose of that monster is sticking right between the third and fourth chakras —between the animal-nature chakras, the first three, and the fourth, at the level of the heart, of spiritual transformation—and that nose is pointing to a platform on which is sitting the baboon, Thoth, the symbol of Hermes, the guide of souls into immortality.

P: I didn't know the Egyptians had the chakras at all.

JC: No one did—but there it is. Another image which we have from India is the five sheaths that enwrap the *Atman*. The outermost is the sheath of food, next the sheath of breath, which activates the food sheath, oxidizes it, and brings life. The next is the sheath of mind, which is attached to these first two sheaths. Then there is a deep break, followed by the sheath of wisdom—this is the wisdom of the body, the wisdom of nature, protoplasm, the body and the cell, where the transcendent energy that shapes everything comes pouring into the world. And beneath that is the sheath of bliss. And then you look at the sarcophagus of Tutankhamun where there are three rectangular boxes enclosing the great sarcophagus, and the sarcophagus is of two sheaths: an outer one of wood inlaid with gold and lapis-lazuli and an inner one of pure gold—the sheath of bliss.

P: I'd like to go back to the American Indians. How do they speak of the process of awakening?

JC: In initiation. As a matter of fact, in this book that I'm now writing—when you just now rang my doorbell, I was right in the middle of a sentence about an American Indian initiation: an initiation myth having to do with two boys—twin heroes—born of a virgin. Their father is the Sun. Monsters are troubling the land, and the boys—one a warrior and the other a medicine man—journey to their father the Sun to get weapons. The father puts them through a series of four terrible tests, and when they survive these tests, he initiates them, tells them what their true names are. That's it—the awakening to the inward self, to the knowledge of who you truly are.

And here's another kind of initiation. Back in the 1830s, a young painter from Harvard named George Catlin went out to the West when it was real Indian country. His full-face portraits, in which the eyes seemed to follow one around, gave him a tremendous reputation among the Indians as a magician, and as a magician they admitted him to some of their hidden ceremonies. One of them was the one that we have all seen pictured, in which the young braves are hung up with skewers through their chest muscles and whirled around and around till they faint and are dropped to the ground. The point of that procedure, Catlin reported, was that "they should learn to rest well in God." No fear. Knud Rasmussen got a similar answer from an old shaman somewhere in the Arctic. A shaman, of course, is in a very anomalous position with his people. He is the one who has waked up, but he is in danger because people are afraid of him and tend to blame him for anything that goes wrong. So the shaman has to invent ways to hold the people off—ways that often involve a lot of make-believe and fakery. Rasmussen asked this old man up there in Alaska if there was anything he really believed in. "Oh yes," the old man said, "I believe in the soul of the universe. I hear it. It's a voice that you can't hear with people around. You can find it only in silence and solitude. And what it says is: 'Do not be afraid of the universe.'" That's big stuff! Some of those old boys really had it.

P: It seems there are clues about the need to awaken in all the traditional teachings, and even in the fairy tales. How do you understand the Sleeping Beauty?

JC: That's psychological rather than metaphysical. This is the story of the little girl who balks on the threshold of womanhood. So she stops there and has to be kissed awake by the consort whom she has refused to face. The Frog Prince is another one like that. This time it's the boy who is afraid to grow up. An old witch has turned him into a frog and there he is, asleep at the bottom of the pool. A girl loses her golden ball, which is symbolic of her soul—gold is the incorruptible metal and the sphere is the perfect shape of the soul. The ball rolls into the pool and awakens him. He comes up to the surface of the water and that little romance begins there between the unblocked boy and the unblocked girl.

P: The girl was blocked too?

JC: She was blocked and that was why she lost the golden ball. She's melancholy, given to brooding. She likes to sit where else but at the edge of the forest—between the dark world of the unconscious and the real world of light.

P: But don't both these stories perhaps also suggest the awakening of a new consciousness as well as the sexual thing? Isn't it possible that the Sleeping Beauty and the Prince and the frog and the girl represent parts of ourselves?

JC: I suppose you could say that. But that's not the way I read them. Take the three old women in the Sleeping Beauty story. They're obviously the Fates saying, "You have to grow up." It's a question of facing up to one's fate. It's the same thing that Paris had to face when he sat in judgment of the three great goddesses. Jane Harrison has shown this very well. In some of the earlier ceramic representations of the scene you see Hermes waking up the sleeping Paris to face those three goddesses. Each one represents a destiny. Each one offers a prize if he will choose her. Aphrodite's prize is to be a great lover, Hera's to be a great ruler, and Athene's to be an achieving hero. The moment of awakening is also the moment of choice. And this is how the alchemists understood the scene. They picture it as the challenge to Paris to wake up, face the goddesses, choose, and discover his life.

P: Is this waking motif present in other aspects of alchemy?

JC: That's what it's all about. It's the same as the Manichean idea that the Divine Light is enclosed in darkness. We live in that double world of darkness imprisoning the Light, and waking is breaking through and releasing the Light. You find the same idea in *The Gospel According to Thomas*, where Jesus says: "The Kingdom of Heaven is spread upon the earth and men do not see it." Wake up! It's here in front of your face!

The Only Freedom

An Interview with Helen M. Luke

From PARABOLA Vol. 11, No. 2, "Mirrors"

> Founder of the Apple Farm Community, **Helen Luke** was a Jungian counselor
> and writer. Her books include **Kaleidoscope: The Way of Woman and Other
> Essays, Such Stuff as Dreams Are Made On,** and **The Laughter at the Heart of
> Things** (all PARABOLA Books). This interview was conducted by **Parabola** editor
> Lorraine Kisly.

PARABOLA: There seem to be many ways of looking at the question of mirrors.

HELEN LUKE: The first thing that strikes me is the word *reflection*—that's what a
mirror is. It reflects back to you. Reflection comes from an
instinct within us and it is the only instinct that is solely human.
It is that which creates consciousness. C. G. Jung says that
"Consciousness is part of the divine life process. In other
words, God becomes manifest in the human act of reflection."
And now I begin to remember various stories about mirrors.

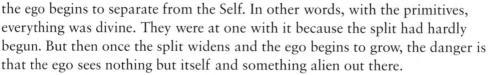

All of our behavior, everything that happens to us is a
reflection, is a mirror image, so to speak, of what is going
on within. And reflection means a bending back. So that
when that human art of reflection upon what you see begins,
the ego begins to separate from the Self. In other words, with the primitives,
everything was divine. They were at one with it because the split had hardly
begun. But then once the split widens and the ego begins to grow, the danger is
that the ego sees nothing but itself and something alien out there.

P: What you say opens up four or five questions at once. I am wondering, for
example, how can we speak of truth or of meaning, if what we perceive is
what we project?

HL: It's the only way that we can become aware of it.

P: The whole world mirrors back to us what we project.

HL: Yes, but let's be clear about projection. We don't do it. Everything that is unconscious is projected. You can't help it—we live in the dimension of causality, and we have to see it out there before we can come back to experiencing the oneness of the primitive or the child—but come back, through reflection—consciously. Charles Williams has a wonderful phrase. He says, "Flesh knows, but spirit knows it knows." And what it knows is the same thing, but in order to be conscious you have to know that you know. And so it seems to me that we start looking in the mirror and then possibly turn into a Narcissus who sees nothing but his own ego and who becomes identified with it. You know the story of Narcissus, that the reason he fell in love with the image of himself was that he would not respond to any of the nymphs who were longing to have him make love to them. Not only Echo, but all the others, too. So he was stuck with falling in love with his own image, and he saw nothing but that. But there are also stories of people who see truth in mirrors—even the mirror of the stepmother in "Snow White." She saw the truth, that she wasn't as beautiful as her stepdaughter.

P: Yes, exactly.

HL: She was at least able to see and recognize that. But not Narcissus. So he just shriveled away and died.

P: So there are two kinds of mirrors.

HL: The mirror is the same, but it's the attitude which differs. You see, if you look at the image without reflection of any kind, then all you see is your ego. That's why it's so vital to start with seeing your shadow. Because if you don't see that, all you see is your superficial ego and you go through life identified with totally impulsive behavior. But if you reflect upon what you see, you begin to be objective—just begin, at first about your own darkness, and then about other individual people and so on, instead of seeing darkness everywhere else.

P: Is the shadow a kind of mirror?

HL: Oh, very much so. It is the mirror of the opposite within you.

P: Is it the mirror of the ego?

HL: The shadow, yes, is the dark side of the ego. But it's been repressed. And you see, when a thing is repressed it becomes very powerful, and is always projected out there, on somebody else or something else or circumstances or whatever it may be. But reflection is not an act of thought only. It's an attitude. It's an attitude which makes a beginning of objectivity possible.

P: Reflection is a mysterious activity. It's not just rational analysis. It has to be activated—something has to be active inside in order for us to have this capacity.

HL: Well, we all have the capacity. That is man's capacity. No animal reflects. It is a wondrous instinct. The moment we are no longer whole, in order to go on that long journey of Return, after the Fall into the knowledge of good and evil, we have to continue to reflect upon everything that happens to us or that we do or that we feel. And when we can become objective about our ego, when we can relate to our ego as objectively as to anything or anybody else, that's when the next step, the final thing, comes to those who get that far. For most of us, it will be just moments, when the subject and the object are one.

Reflection is the conscious balancing of the opposites. It's a refusal to repress one in order to live in the other whichever it may be—the dark or the light. And that is the only thing that breaks through the fog of the emotions, when an emotion takes one over. It stops being impulsive, and it becomes spontaneous—the spirit knowing it's spontaneous—not regressing to the child who is simply natural and unknowing, but becoming in full awareness "as a little child."

P: I wonder if there is a more unnatural act than welcoming contradiction. It seems so difficult.

HL: An extremely difficult act. But it is the essential one.

P: It's the last thing one wishes to undergo, the experience of internal contradiction.

HL: Unless we live all our lives in the torment of the contradictions, as C. G. Jung insists, then we're not human. We can't become whole. If you're stuck, and you don't know what to do, stuck between two opposites, and you allow them each to live *within* you, then a small transformation of the ego takes place. It becomes related to the Self instead of identifying with it.

P: It seems that this is perhaps one of the paths towards the almost impossible idea that one could relate to the ego objectively. The bearing of contradiction is a kind of tool which pries apart the identification with the ego.

HL: Yes, indeed, it is so.

P: An indirect method, but it seems to have that effect.

HL: Jung says—as I've quoted already—"God becomes manifest in the human act of reflection." That's to say, our God images are what we see in our mirrors. Narcissus' God image was his own ego. But the Zen mirror, which they say must be utterly free of dust, reveals the experience of the whole. That's the whole point of Zen, isn't it? All the contradictions—you can't put it into words at all. It's a sudden breakthrough.

P: They use contradiction as a tool, also.

HL: Very much so. All their koans are contradictions unsolvable by reason. As I was going on to say, you have a conflict, you reflect, you simply bear it, and suddenly you glimpse the truth which unites the opposites; it breaks through. You are then released to act. And then you must not stop. That's what we get into all the time, isn't it? We think we've had a breakthrough, and now everything is going to be lovely and we're going to feel good. But on the contrary, you must then start again on the next conflict, quite soon. And then there's another. So that one has to learn to rejoice in the conflict. Which doesn't mean be happy!

P: It would require an understanding of the situation that you're in to go on in this way—an understanding that this is something you undertake or undergo voluntarily for the sake of something higher.

HL: Yes. Somebody once wrote, "Free will is simply to do gladly that which one must do." I always liked that. It can be the last thing you feel in your personal emotions—but then, emotion has always something unconscious in it. Not that we mustn't have emotions, we must. That's the mirror, we've got to look into it. There is always paradox, isn't there, in any inner truth?

There is an instance in J. R. R. Tolkien's *The Lord of the Rings* with Galadriel's mirror. In Lothlorien when Sam and Frodo pause there before the great journey, Galadriel takes them to look into her mirror, which is a bowl of water, because she feels they're pure enough in heart. Of course, a mirror is always symbolically the water of the unconscious. It's looking into the unconscious. And Sam sees the future. He sees what's going to happen at home, all the awful things that are going to happen. He's in a terrible state and he says, "I must go home at once." And she says, in effect, "What you see there are things that may or may not happen in that way, in the future. But if you turn aside from your present task and try to put something right that you see predicted, then most certainly you will only increase the danger."

One simply has to stick to the next thing that one must do. And then of course in the end when the hobbits return they find that situation and set it right. That little bit about the mirror has always stuck in my mind since I read it. It's a cure for many fears.

P: I suppose it's obvious, but it struck me when Jung said that most people think of consciousness as consciousness of the ego-personality.

HL: Yes, of course it's not really consciousness, because it excludes the Self, it excludes the unconscious as a reality.

P: What is consciousness? We use the word self-consciousness, and mean by it what we know about ourselves in our egos.

HL: Yes, and in a way it's true. It's what the ego can express in his or her way of life—it is the Self becoming conscious in every individual, but when used in *that* way it is distorted to mean the identification of the self with rational thinking, which is not really consciousness at all.

P: So consciousness resides in the ego?

HL: Yes. But this is very interesting because it seems to me I have seen so often that people go through a long period of a kind of ego research into their motives. This is the analytic stage. But the time comes when you have to stop and that can be very, very difficult, because one of the most difficult things is to give up one's neurosis. As long as you have a neurosis you can repress things, and you can find excuses. But when comes the time when you *could* give it up, this is when many people break down. They won't. They can't. It's a prop. A whole different attitude can arise when you accept that neurosis itself as part of your destiny in life. And then it won't be neurosis anymore.

You see, reflection takes you *contra natura*—against nature—but there must come a time when nature and the work of the spirit are not split apart. You *know* that you know.

P: There's this capacity—to see, to observe. You were saying before that it's instinctive, or in any case that the capacity seems to be born with the human.

HL: I think Marie-Louise von Franz said in one of her fairy tale books that in her view, the religious instinct in a baby—religious used in the real sense—is stronger even than hunger. That is something, isn't it?

P: Yes, when you think about the lack of nourishment for that instinct. And what are the consequences if it's not fed at all?

HL: You can see one consequence in the enormous numbers of young people who commit suicide. It's just that they cannot stand the awful weight of the collective darkness. And there's only one answer—that each one of us recognizes the responsibility of carrying our little bit of darkness—not to try to carry the whole thing personally. And that can save somebody a thousand miles away, as the Chinese say—not because we try to save the world, but because we live out our life stories with the utmost devotion to that which is not the ego but includes it.

P: How have we gotten to this state where we're only in the ego and totally denying the shadow? Is it a new state for humanity?

HL: Oh, no. It began with Cain and Abel.

P: It seems more dangerous now than ever.

HL: Perhaps it isn't. Perhaps it's no more dangerous fundamentally than it ever has been. The trouble nowadays I think is that we know everything that's going on in every corner of the world almost as soon as it's happened. It's created a much greater threat of mass thinking. And that's the monster. Then the individual is totally lost in the mass. But there are signs of a great many individuals appearing now in a true search for meaning. The world of subatomic physics is a new exciting mirror as it approaches the world of the spirit, and the awareness of the unity of matter and spirit is dawning in many.

P: I'm still thinking about this faculty which can tolerate the dark side, as if there's something which is caught now—caught in the ego, caught in projections, caught in the unconscious. What is that faculty which needs to be freed?

HL: Well, it is the sense of God. One's central motive in life is really one's God, isn't it? "Where your treasure is, there will your heart be also."

P: The ego is a mirror. It's not "I." But it's something through which "I" can become conscious, eventually.

HL: Become a unique individual.

P: It's also the ego which can become aware of the unconscious.

HL: Oh, yes, it's only the ego. That's the importance of it. What has to be sacrificed is not the ego itself, but the ego's demand to be first, to be the Self. And you know there are those who are inflated and identified with the Self, as though the ego were the Self—but there are also those who identify with the negative side, and who are forever really playing God by saying how terrible and awful they are. Instead of recognizing that yes, indeed, of course I have awful things in me, but that too is not me. The "good" and the "bad" are neither of them you and yet they are both a reality in your life and a mirror for the Self. When you recognize this you no longer are impelled to act without reflection on every impulse. Which doesn't mean that you get rid of your impulses, which are the stuff of life, but that having reflected even for two seconds on them, they don't possess you. Your choice of action remains.

P: That's a kind of a freedom.

HL: The only freedom.

A sudden recognition can be another sort of mirror—and recognition means to know again. I remember, when I was first learning of Jung's work, I got hold of about the most difficult book at that time. *The Psychology of the Unconscious,* it was called. That's the only time of my life I've sat up all night long reading. And I just had the feeling that this was something I had always known. I didn't understand a word, but I thought it was something that was going to change my life because I'd always known it. That is a sort of seeing, isn't it, like seeing in the mirror, "in a glass darkly." It is true of all of us, that we all know these things, and then somebody speaks in a new kind of language that says just what you've been longing for, and you recognize it.

P: The mirror which tells the truth about you.

HL: And then it takes the rest of one's life to begin to know what it's all about.

P: I'm thinking of the messengers from above—Christ, Buddha—as a kind of mirror, also. A kind of perfect mirror.

HL: The mirror free of dust. Because they are one in themselves, God, the incarnate unity. They are also images of what a human being could be.

P: If you know the ego-personality of someone very, very well, can you construct their shadow? Will you know what will show up? Is it a kind of reverse mirror?

HL: If you heard a few dreams, you'd know the kind of thing, of course. You mean could one intuit what kind of darkness would be there? Oh, yes. Surely you could too. If you meet someone who's very, very sweet and never will risk hurting anybody's feelings, wouldn't you know that underneath there must be a venomous kind of thing?

P: Perhaps.

HL: If someone is working with you, then it becomes clear quickly. It's one's business to listen but never to go ahead of what they're able to take. It's a very slow business. There are people who are carrying dark things that don't belong to them at all. To go back to what we were saying before about young people's suicide, it kind of dropped into my mind that they are almost like the Holy Innocents slaughtered by the Herod in our culture. They're often the most sensitive and beautiful children, who simply can't take the collective darkness. We can think of it as a kind of sacrificial thing whereby something is saved, as the Christ child was saved.

P: How does one begin to admit one's own darkness, and separate what is one's own from what one has taken on? They're both dark, they're both unconscious.

HL: How you know the difference? It's very difficult, I think. If we can stick with just tiny instances of how we behaved to somebody or how we've reacted emotionally to something or other, we can see where the shadow has an open door. And then in comes the collective element and one feels swamped. And this of course is what happens in schizophrenia. There's no protection at all. There's no definition of where the ego begins and ends. I knew a girl once who every time she read about a murder in New York—she lived in California—she was sure she was responsible, because she'd had an evil thought. Now there is a sense in which this is true. We are all responsible for the state of the world, of the unconscious, but not in the personal sense. And we have to recognize that all we can do is take care of our minute share. It's the same when you've been very badly treated by someone. All right, that's their business. But there is always, even if it's only very small, one's own part in it. And we can attend to that. You can find it again and again through the mirror of your behavior, or the mirror of your emotions. That is reflection again, an active reflection of your emotional reactions can turn into response instead of reaction. That means a conscious response rather than an automatic reaction.

P: There are examples in relationships with people when you get a reaction from someone else, which shows you something about yourself which you've not been able to see.

HL: Yes. But what a temptation to say, "Well that's just him or her."

The real guilt is if you refuse to see what the mirror is telling you. If you are sincere, you may go bumbling on and make the mistake several times over, but in the end it will come back at you and come back at you. You will be meeting it everywhere until you do get the right thing.

P: I think everyone has experienced a situation which repeats and repeats, as though one attracts the same situation over and over again.

HL: The unconscious is trying to tell you it has a message for you.

P: A mirror doubles the impressions and it seems that if you are able to reflect upon what's happening in a moment, the impressions there are doubled as well. It isn't just happening, but you're aware of it happening and somehow the whole picture has another dimension.

HL: Literally another dimension. And that's the whole thing. And finally the fourth dimension which completes the one world, which is outside time.

P: It's clear that an analyst might function as a mirror. In what sense?

HL: The situation in analysis is contained. You see, it's almost like the mirror is . . . it's like pouring water into a bowl, a container. And a person can look into it. Simone Weil said the only purpose of any education should be to train attention. I like that. We're still learning it.

P: That is the material of reflection: attention. Isn't it? And that is a very mysterious element.

HL: Yes, mysterious to our minds because it is not a rational thinking effort. It is living in the moment: past and future become one. The basic meaning of the word *attend* is to be present. It is not equivalent to the being present of nature—there is a specifically human content. Attention involves seeing, listening, caring, and courtesy, which arise from the inclusion of the human act of intention and concentration beyond thought. Thus, the subject and the object are one. In those moments, the mirror is clear.

Worshipping Illusions

An Interview with Marion Woodman

From PARABOLA Vol. 12, No. 2, "Addiction"

Marion Woodman was trained as an analyst at the Jung Institute in Zürich and lectures in the United States and Canada. She is the author of a number of books on the psychology and attitudes of women, including **Addiction to Perfection: The Still Unravished Bride** (Inner City), **Dancing in the Flames: The Dark Goddess in the Transformation of Consciousness** (Shambhala), and **Bone: Dying into Life** (Viking). This interview was conducted by **Parabola** editor Lorraine Kisly.

PARABOLA: The title of one of your books, *Addiction to Perfection,* raises a great many questions. I wonder if you could explain a little about what that title means.

MARION WOODMAN: Well, it comes in part from the situation in which parents have a concept of what the perfect child would be— perfect athlete, perfect scholar, when one hundred per- cent achievement is the goal. The parents are trapped by this ideal, and their whole life is centered around per- formance. The child then learns how to perform and has an idealized vision of what he or she should be. Anything that doesn't fit in with that ideal has to be pushed back, has to be annihilated, really. As a result, whatever is human in the child, whatever is "dirty"—sexuality, and the plain, ordinary world of the body—the child expe- riences as not part of the perfect ideal. Spontaneity—just the natural anger or natural joy even, or the natural love of rocks and mud—is blocked, and the child gets the idea on some level that he or she is unlovable. "Whoever I am in the reality of my being is not lovable," the child concludes.

Natural being is repressed, and performance becomes everything. In any given situation a person subject to this repression will figure out whom to please and then perform in order to please that person, and their own reality is not present in the performance. People begin to live for an ideal—there's nothing else to live for. But if you are living for an ideal, and driving yourself as hard as you can to be perfect—at your job or as a mother or as the perfect wife—you lose the natural, slow rhythm of life. There's just a rushing, trying to attain the ideal. The slower pace of the beat of the earth, the state where you simply *are*, is forgotten.

P: It was forgotten long ago, really.

MW: Long ago. The parents have forgotten it, and the grandparents have forgotten it. It's a cultural situation. In its worst form, it's what happened in Nazi Germany. They sought to create a race of supermen, and they were guided by an ideal of this kind. Anything that did not fit in with that rigid concept was killed. I am now in the position to hear the dreams of people suffering from subjection to this kind of ideal, and their dreams are full of Nazi concentration camps. They are living their lives in a Nazi concentration camp. In these dreams, soldiers are killing all the women, baby girls are being raped, animals and women are having their limbs torn off. You see, the instinct is being distorted as well.

In the feminine side of our being is a much slower, less rational side, a part that moves in a much more spontaneous, natural, and receptive way, a part that accepts life as it is without judgment.

For me, *perfection* is a patriarchal word that splits everything into contraries: black or white. You are then living in constant conflict, and integration is not possible. Even the language is split, so that I find people who cannot endure words such as *masculine* and *feminine*. They go into a rage at the word *masculine,* or a word like *penetration,* or words like *phallic thrust,* because they have been so outraged by what they call "the masculine principle." I don't call it the masculine principle; I call it the power principle— that's what it really is. But certainly, in the patriarchy of the business world and in many homes, what's operating is power—"You be like I want you to be," and "I love you so much that I know exactly what you ought to be," and "You will do it, or I will not accept you. I will reject you." And so people are living in terror of rejection.

P: It leads to compulsive behavior, and then the fury at the denial of most of themselves is projected back out onto their parents?

MW: Or on to men, or on to the culture. People think of the culture as being violent—they have a great fear of violence, but the violence is inside as well. They are afraid of what would happen if they let that rage out. They feel they would actually destroy other people if they did, so they have to keep it down.

P: Is the root of this situation a mental one? It seems to come from an idea in the mind that compels people to live according to a certain picture of themselves.

MW: It's an image of what life should be but is not. So it's worship of an illusion. It simply is not real. You can see that with an anorexic, for example. She has an image of what her body should be, and she treats herself as a Nazi officer would have treated her in a concentration camp. She kills her femininity in order to force herself into a rigid ideal, which is delusion.

P: The taking in of this ideal from the outside is so destructive to the individual—and yet it is taken in and embraced with gusto. Why do we embrace it if it is so self-destructive and causes so much suffering?

MW: If you are raised in a home that is based on the power principle, that's the only reality you know. You have no other world to judge by. Terrified of being left alone, the only reality you understand is pleasing other people, and you have within yourself no individual standpoint. You don't even know such a thing exists—that's the tragedy. And then you treat other people the way you were treated, so you raise your kids the same way. You know it's all wrong that essentially you are not happy, but you have no other model for reality, so the pattern is repeated.

P: Is there anyone who is really free from this? No matter what, the parent will always have some idea of what the child ought to be like.

MW: Well, I'm sure there are some parents who can love the child for who the child is.

P: They would have to be parents who have first of all been able to love themselves.

MW: That's right. That's where it starts. You have to forgive yourself first for being human, because to be human is to have lots of faults; so you have to forgive, and then the love flows in. "Forgiveness" is the crucial word. If you are brought up on ideals but know you have human failings and unacceptable qualities, you have to forgive yourself for being human, and it is through this forgiveness that you forgive others. But that is so difficult to do in our society, because we are not being loved for ourselves so we hide our worst faults.

Even in analysis, we will hide our worst faults, and if we begin to sense that we are being loved, even with all our ugliness and darkness, there is an immense fear and resistance, because we feel vulnerable, and suddenly the word *trust* starts to come in. And we are terrified of trust; we are terrified to make ourselves vulnerable. So the move into forgiveness is an immense leap. People will move to a point of trust, and then the unconscious reaction is one of terror, because they are wide open, they can be struck down. So then you have to wait. And there's another opening to more love, and then again the terror comes in. And it's the body that's terrified. Many people begin to realize at that point that their body was rejected. If they engage in depth massage or inner work in the body, the agony of the body begins to come up.

P: I'm trying to envisage this process going on outside of analysis. Could it?

MW: Sure.

P: In a relationship with someone? So often the situation is unconscious; how do you begin to shed light on it?

MW: Many of the letters that I receive are from people who are not in analysis, but they say "Thank God for this light on what I'm trying to do. I could never see the meaning of what I was trying to do, but now I think I have some idea." They are beginning to realize that they live trying to please others. They are trying to start to live from who they are, what their needs are, what their real fears are, what their real emotions locked in their muscles are. They are trying to experience themselves as body and soul, so that others will have to respond to them in their own reality. And that takes love. You may not like what the person is saying to you at all, particularly if you have thought of them in a certain way and all of a sudden they start saying things they never said in their lives before. If, for example, they start expressing rage or contempt, it can be very threatening. But I think that's where it starts. The person acts more and more from his or her own individual standpoint. Now that standpoint will change constantly. Gradually you become conscious of the emotions in the body supporting what you are saying, and you experience them as having substance. Instead of just speaking from the neck up, you discover what's in the body. It seems a lot of people are cut off at the neck, so that they talk from the head. Meanwhile, something completely different can be going on below the neck. There's a real split inside.

P: What you have called "inner civil war."

MW: Inner civil war. And that's why so many people try to drown themselves in the addiction. As soon as the rage begins to come up, they start eating or drinking or spending money, or they turn to sex or an obsessive relationship. Or gambling, or TV. Anything that will block out consciousness. The addictive substance acts as a soporific, and gradually they sink into unconsciousness.

From my point of view, in each case you have to try to figure out what the addictive substance means symbolically. Otherwise, it will hold an almost religious significance. Now that most people do not have a religious focus, the religious focus will go on to something material. They may think it's food they want, for example, because they experience themselves as starving. Well, the soul is starving; it's true, because it's not being recognized, and it's being continually starved. They then try to feed it with food, which usually symbolizes the loving mother who can accept them as they are.

P: And you see different substances as having different symbols? Alcohol?

MW: Spirit, the longing for the light; whereas food grounds you, puts you back in the body, alcohol will take you out into the light. I think the positive side of addiction is that many addicts are profoundly religious people. They have immense energy, and they are not satisfied with the world as it is. They think it is a dreadfully cruel, ruthless place, and they want meaning in their lives.

P: So perhaps they feel the need more acutely than others.

MW: Because they have such a driving energy. And they want a god. Now they'd never say that, but they want something bigger than the bread-and-butter world. If that's all there is, it's meaningless. If life is nothing more than driven work, for example, it is not worth living. The alcohol takes them out of the mundane world, temporarily—and then, of course, ultimately it takes them into unconsciousness.

P: It has always seemed to me that addiction had the elements of both avoidance and substitution.

MW: Yes. The avoidance would be the avoidance of the inner civil war, and it's also an avoidance of reality. Reality is too painful if the bottom line is that I am not lovable, that I will be rejected if I am who I am. That is an unbearably painful recognition.

P: But different from the need for another level that you just spoke of.

MW: Yes. One side of it is fear. The other side is that I am looking for a deeper reality.

P: In your book you write that many people are driven to addiction because "there is no collective container for their natural spiritual needs."

MW: It used to be there in the church, for example, where people would enter into the sacred world, surrender to it, leave the sacred world, and take that energy back to the profane world. But they had something to take with them; they had a meaning. Their suffering was given meaning. You can't live with meaningless suffering. So you have avoidance—addicts do not live in the here-and-now. They are always going to stop drinking next Monday, or they're going to stop eating next Monday, but meanwhile eat as much as they can between now and Monday. Everything is going to be all right in the future . . . but here and now? They are never where they are; they are always running, or dreaming about the wonderful past, or the wonderful future. So they are never in the body. The body lives in the present. The body exists right now. But an addict is not in the body, so the body suffers. Uninhabited. And there's where that terrible sense of starvation comes from.

P: The fact that the whole culture is in an addictive state interests me in terms of this lack of meaning. It is as though there is a fundamental human need for meaning that can be as strong as instinctive needs. What could meet that need for those who are alienated from the traditional churches?

MW: Well, I think there are two things here. If you imagine the uninhabited body as sort of an empty hole, you see people try to fill it in different ways. But the soul in the body is left empty. My answer to that is that the real food of the soul is metaphor. The whole world of dreams is a metaphorical, symbolic one. Religion is based on symbol. Art, music, poetry, the whole creative world—the world of the soul—is based on it.

P: So there is a faculty within that understands this world—that lives on it, in fact.

MW: It lives on it—it is as important as food. We simply must have access to that symbolic realm, because we are not animals only, and we are not gods only. Somehow there has to be a bridge between the animal and the divine within, and that is the symbol. Children understand this. They love fairy tales, for example. But in our culture, these are taken away from them very early on. The world of the imagination is repressed, and the soul is left crying.

P: There is an enormous price to pay to keep all of that down.

MW: It won't be held down. Eventually you'll be faced with nightmare. Eventually it will come up. Or it will take a perverse route and say "Give me spirit," and instead of understanding this symbolically, people interpret it concretely: and they start to drink alcohol, which is a concretization of that longing.

P: There's something very hopeful in it when you look at it that way!

MW: I like working with addicts, because they are desperate and they know there is something really wrong. A lot of them wish they were dead. They are on a self-destructive course, and they know it. The world as it is is intolerable, and their lives are intolerable, because they aren't really living their own lives.

P: It seems like more than a problem to "fix." It seems to have a very creative aspect.

MW: It does. Death and resurrection. And they do go through the death. What I see in a broader sense is that the feminine principle, which for centuries has been so denied in our culture, is forcing its way, her way, back in again. If you're an addict, you have got to come to terms with the feminine principle. You've got to feel that slow rhythm—the rhythm of the earth is slow—you have to feel that slowing down, you have to quiet the soul, and you have to surrender, because eventually you have to face the fact that you are not God and you cannot control your life.

P: Something has to surrender; something has to let go and give up.

MW: Power.

P: Now, in most of us who are power-possessed, the instincts governed by our feminine side are pretty primitive. Whatever is repressed in childhood is not very developed. So it comes out in very violent ways—at first, or forever?

MW: At first it will come out in very primitive ways, very challenging ways, and you will find yourself acting like a three-year-old: "These are my rights." People who are trying to find themselves can have very bad manners. If they were in their polite persona, they would never act that way. When that little girl starts to come out, she is wild. But she has to come out.

P: So the feminine is not just the slow benevolent rhythms of the earth— there is also the dark side of the feminine.

MW: The dark side of the feminine is vicious; it's a killer.

P: The devouring mother, Kali.

MW: Yes. Men are terrified of her—and so are women. And that side comes up—that's what's so complicated about it—that side comes up along with the loving Great Mother. If you're trapped in Kali, you are literally paralyzed. You wake up in the morning, and your body just doesn't want to move. Here we have the Medusa that turns people to stone. If they try to do anything creative they become frozen. Or petrified. And that's real. For many people who are trying to do something from themselves for the first time in their life, as soon as that urge is felt and they really start to make a move, the dark mother appears and there is an immense battle. But you have to just keep talking to her, and realize what's happening, and not give up. It takes courage and strength.

P: What is it in people that can face all of those things? The ego is involved in the repression. Is it the ego that can see what is going on? What is it in us? Obviously we have the capacity to do it.

MW: Yes. It would be ego ultimately. But most people have to work very hard to build an ego. Most people are operating on the persona, which is the showpiece, the masquerade. They are performing—they aren't in touch with their real feelings, and in a given situation, they don't know if they are angry or if they want to cry. They are unhappy about not being able to express their emotions and also terrified to do so, because expressing them has led to rejection.

P: So the ego is really the vehicle of consciousness?

MW: It is ego that can recognize what the feelings are, what the inner needs are. From a Jungian point of view, the unconscious is a vast sea where all the complexes are just floating around like onions: mother, father, hero, young child. On the underside is the collective unconscious, on the upper side is the collective in the world, and at the heart of all this there is a pinpoint called the ego, which is trying to filter what's coming through from the unconscious while at the same time trying to deal with the collective. The ego is a filter system that relates to all of reality. But considering the immense buffeting that it's getting from both the unconscious and consciousness, it has a difficult job. It takes a lot of patience to build a strong ego. But the stronger the ego is and the more flexible it is, the more it can allow to come through from the unconscious—and that's where the real wisdom is. But ego is partly in the unconscious and partly in consciousness. It tells us what is real and what is not real. If you didn't have an ego, you might think you were Christ, for example. If the place of the ego is taken over, one becomes possessed.

Actually that is what happens in an addictive state—you become possessed, and the ego is not strong enough to prevent this from happening, even though you know you are destroying yourself. There isn't sufficient ego strength to resist. So the complex takes over. But even there, it could be that the complex is acting out of a longing for the light, or consciousness. As a matter of fact, I see the repression of the feminine principle as the biggest problem on the planet, and since the planet has become a global village, power alone just isn't going to work any more. We will destroy ourselves. So I have enough faith to believe that the feminine is forcing her way into consciousness by means of these addictions. It changes lives, and it could change the whole culture.

P: We were just talking about how there are two aspects of this feminine force, positive and negative.

MW: When I'm talking about the feminine, I'm not talking about a mother principle. Certainly the Great Goddess is a part of this archetype—she is matter, the body. But symbolically the mother principle is based on a full breast giving to a hungry child. The mother has to give, and the child has to take. And this experience, too, can become contaminated by the power principle. Many children fall into an immense guilt, because they don't want to take. But if the mother has identified with the mother principle, the child has to take from her, or else, who is she? The feminine principle, however, is not limited to that.

P: What you just described is a distortion of the feminine?

MW: Well, it's unconscious. No mother would admit she is operating on a power principle when she's giving milk to her baby. And on the one hand she isn't, she's nourishing. But if the stage is reached where the child no longer needs her and says "Look, I don't want your orange juice," and the mother is annihilated by that, then power, or the need for control, is involved. And that causes a distortion of the mother-child relationship, because the child is trapped in guilt.

Feminine consciousness rises out of the mother, and you have to be grounded in that, because without it you'd just be blown away by spirit. Feminine consciousness, as I see it, means going into that grounding and recognizing there who you are as a soul. It has to do with love, with receiving—most of us in this culture are terrified of receiving. It has to do with surrendering to your own destiny, consciously—not just blindly, but recognizing with full consciousness your strengths, your limitations. It gets into a much broader area, because a man's body is also feminine—all matter is feminine. We are talking about a masculine principle and a feminine principle—we are not talking about gender. Men are even farther out of their bodies than women, it seems to me. I've seen men in body workshops where a relaxation exercise is being tried, and the men's bodies are so often terribly rigid—to the point where they cannot lie flat on the floor, the muscles are just chronically locked—trying to be good little boys. They can't let the muscles relax. If you think of matter as an aspect of the feminine principle another dimension is revealed.

P: The masculine principle—or spirit—can't live anywhere except in the body. It has to be received by something.

MW: Exactly—it has to be received. And there's where consciousness comes in. You can't put spirit into dense matter. Matter is dark; it's obtuse. There has to be a consciousness to receive spirit. The way I'm understanding it—more and more from dreams—is that consciousness exists in matter, and that consciousness opens to receive spirit.

P: It develops in the process of being open to the materiality of my body, and emotions, and thoughts, and so on?

MW: By being aware of it, yes, and also by being aware of the world of symbol.

P: Where did the power principle come from? Is it a distortion of spirit?

MW: Very distorted—and we have to remember that women are trapped in this power principle just as much as men. Matriarchs are very often more authoritarian than men. What I would say is that in the hero-consciousness of the Greeks, the hero was fighting unconsciousness and trying to get a little glimmer of consciousness. For two thousand years there has been an attempt to become more and more conscious, and the hero archetype has ruled—in the Western world, anyway.

P: But you're not speaking of a very developed, complete form of consciousness, are you?

MW: Absolutely not, because it fell under the sway of an unconscious desire for power. In terms of the evolution of our culture, the worship of goddesses in the prehistoric past gradually shifted to the worship of gods—a movement from lunar to solar consciousness. Now what's happening is that people are conscious of the power of the mother and the father complexes, and they are saying, "Who am I?" We are moving into an adolescent period, leaving behind the power of those two great archetypes and trying to move into what in an individual life looks like adolescence; and adolescents are pretty confused.

They are dependent on the parents, and they don't want to be. And we are trapped by the complexes. We know what we're trapped in, and we want to get out. So we keep falling back in, and pulling out. That conflict is going on. It happens in the individual as he or she matures, and I see it in terms of the macrocosm as well.

P: So you see this as a critical point in history.

MW: Absolutely; if we don't make the critical transition into adulthood, we may very well destroy ourselves. We are adolescents with a hydrogen bomb and without a sense of the love that can use that energy creatively. I would say, however, that the addiction keeps a person in touch with the god—what I mean by this is that as in AA, for example, the first thing you have to admit is that you can't control your desire for alcohol, and you have to surrender to a higher power. At the very point of the vulnerability is where the surrender takes place —that is where the god enters. The god comes in through the wound. If you've ever been an addict, you know that you can always be an addict again, so it's at that point that the energy, if opened to, becomes available again and again.

P: Something has to give up in order for that to come in.

MW: Yes, here again we are back to the idea of consciousness in the body that has to open to spirit.

P: We spoke of addiction, for example to alcohol, where the alcohol represents on a low level the spirit. What happens when the addiction is taken away? Where does it go?

MW: I do think it's possible, with an addiction, to start living your life in terms of negatives: "I won't drink." And the danger, with some alcoholics at any rate, is that they get stopped on "I will not drink." But you can't live your life in those terms. They are still obsessed with alcohol—it's still going on. It's true of any kind of addict. You may stop the addictive behavior, but as long as your mind is in that rut, it's still trapped.

P: So the surrender to a "higher power" needs to continue, the openness needs to continue beyond the initial phase of stopping the addictive behavior.

MW: I think the members of AA understand this very well—you have to go through those Twelve Steps. Every addictive person has to keep working at it every day. That's what I mean about addiction keeping you in close contact with the god. You have to be careful not to make another addiction. One needs to hold that container open and live life rich and full.

P: I don't think there is anyone who doesn't have areas of addiction in them.

MW: Certainly most people do.

P: If there are, it doesn't happen by itself, does it?

MW: It doesn't happen by itself, I agree. And no one is entirely free.

P: Even if they feel quite innocent of addiction of any kind—even if it's not overt.

MW: You have to keep growing to the day you die. Otherwise you regress. There's no such thing as stasis.

P: This idea of stasis is one of the ideas that has interested us. There's no such thing as stasis, and yet there seems to be a tremendously strong wish to stay where one is, and not to move. Why?

MW: It's fear. You see in addicts the compulsion to wish to keep things fixed. They are natural lovers of ritual. They create their own rituals, and the addiction will take place around that ritual. But it's a perverted ritual—it carries them into unconsciousness instead of into consciousness. It's a perverted religion, it really is. A ritual should take you into a much broader, richer experience, and every time you go through a ritual you should contact that deepest, divine part of yourself and open to something new. If the ritual leads you into unconsciousness, you regress and become more and more deeply trapped in rigidity. If you have no personal standpoint and no boundaries, you don't dare to open.

P: It's almost as though there is an ontological imperative to grow—and if you don't, as you say, there is no standing still, only regression.

MW: You slip back or you die.

P: I think as people get older, it starts to become evident that either they become more developed or they become caricatures of themselves. It seems that many people are suffering from a refusal of the fact that they have to grow.

MW: We're back to the fear of annihilation again. People are terrified of death.

P: So they'll commit suicide first.

MW: Yes, they will. It's true. Life is a series of deaths and rebirths. You outgrow patterns, you outgrow people, you outgrow work. But if you are frightened and do not have a flexible personality, when you have to face the death of what you've always known, you are pitched into terror. That's where the addiction will really hit. Some people will cure themselves of an addiction, and then ten years later their husband or wife will die, and they have to go on to a new life and they are terrified. They have to retire, or they have to go to a new job, and the fear comes in. Well, they have to let the past die and move into a new life, or what can happen is that they turn to the old addiction. And the addiction will throw them into unconsciousness. They can't make the move, so they will get back into the addictive object or behavior and throw themselves into unconsciousness.

What is so interesting about that, is that they will so often repeat their own birth pattern. By which I mean that you can think about death and rebirth in terms of a birth canal: you are going to say good-bye to the womb and go into a new life. When people enter that "birth canal," they repeat the original birth trauma.

P: This is different for different people?

MW: Oh, of course. People who are born premature will try to go ahead of themselves: they'll always be two or three steps ahead of where they really are. Caesarean births are terrified of confrontation, usually. They've never confronted the initial struggle. People whose mothers were drugged are the ones most likely to fall into an addiction. They tend to be quite passive—waiting for someone to do something at a moment of difficulty. But the fear is the outstanding thing—though it can take any number of bodily symptoms.

P: How, in that state of terror, does one hold oneself open, realizing that its simply one part, not all of you?

MW: It's very important to realize it's only a part. And I think that most people in those birth passages do need support. It's very painful, and a really good friend, or several, can really help—even though you have to do your own work alone, too.

P: This is only one part of really difficult and serious work on oneself that needs to go on. I think it is carried on in living religious traditions and, in recent times, partly in analysis. But analysis is expensive, and many people today feel estranged from religion. How much of this serious work can go on outside of a structure and without contact with someone who knows more than you do, who is more developed than you are? Can a person on their own go very far toward this openness? Certainly the world around us doesn't seem to be of much help.

MW: Do you know the story of the hundredth monkey? I can't tell it to you exactly, but it concerns a situation that was observed on a group of islands near Japan where a few monkeys began washing potatoes before eating them. While the younger ones quickly took up this practice, the older members became more and more frightened and restless. Eventually a few more began till the "hundredth monkey" started. A sort of critical level was achieved, and then, not only all the monkeys on that island, but all the monkeys on the other islands, unconnected, started washing their potatoes as well.

P: Here we get into deep water!

MW: It's an amazing thing, but when one person makes the breakthrough, a movement starts in other people's unconscious. I think that there is such a thing as a cultural move toward consciousness. Certainly when one person in a room is more conscious, it changes the consciousness of everyone in that room. And in a family, if one person is coming into consciousness, everyone in the household is going to be changed.

Something is happening on a large scale—there are radical changes in male-female relationships, and there is an enormous interest in spirit and matter in the fields of science, psychology, and biology. I think many people are doing a lot of inner work; they are really trying to understand what is going on inside themselves. A lot of people are using dance to try to connect with the body. There is an interest in painting, in creating for yourself, in contacting nature. More and more people are trying to save nature from patriarchal exploitation. I know many people who are keeping journals. Many people are writing down their dreams and reconnecting with their inner self. They are questioning and bringing themselves to consciousness, and no matter how they are doing it, they are contacting that symbolic world. That's how I see it. And without that, the addicts are right, life isn't worth living.

Recovering a Common Language

An Interview with Kathleen Raine

From PARABOLA Vol. 8, No. 3, "Words of Power"

Poet, philosopher, editor, and scholar, **Kathleen Raine** is a British writer well-known for her concern with spiritual quest. A self-described neo-Platonist and symbolist poet in the tradition of Yeats, Coleridge, and Blake, she is the author of eight books of verse, a three-volume autobiography, and a seminal study of the philosophic and religious sources of Blake. Dr. Raine lives in London, where she edits **Temenos,** a journal devoted to the "Arts of the Imagination." This interview was conducted for **Parabola** by Alice van Buren and Ken Krushel.

ALICE VAN BUREN: You have written that the problem for any serious artist or educator is to recreate a common language for the communication of spiritual knowledge.

KATHLEEN RAINE: It is a problem. We don't have a common language because we don't have a common view of the universe we're living in. We don't share premises anymore. There is a common language for those who hold a secular, humanist, materialist, positivist view of the world. They have a common language and are very happy with it. But those of us who feel a change of premises taking place have to reestablish a common language not based on the premises of materi-

alism which have held for the past three hundred years. I don't think we can resurrect any of the traditions in quite their old forms. We can't become Zen

Buddhists or honorary Hindus or even go back to the old Christian theological terms as such—or in my case to the Platonic tradition. But we can reexplore these civilizations, which did have a spiritual basis, and retranslate their ideas into forms appropriate to the present.

AVB: What forms can we look to for this new-old language?

KR: We won't find them. We won't find ready-made the culture which it is our task to create. But we will recreate our culture by going back to the roots. That means a lot of hard work. Blake did this. He bypassed the materialist epoch of Bacon, Newton, and Locke, and went back to neo-Platonism, to Boehme. He found the roots, and they resurfaced again in his work. This has happened in this century many times. The Theosophical movement is a reassembling of the threads. Yeats studied Swedenborg, Blake, Theosophy, neo-Platonism, Buddhism, the Noh theater, and finally Hinduism; he scanned the horizon for those sources which are available to us today. It's for us to rediscover the threads which were once in our hands.

KEN KRUSHEL: If each generation has to reexamine these roots, isn't there a danger of the language or idiom changing too frequently?

KR: It is changing too frequently. There is a confusion of tongues.

KK: Such as Freudianism, Jungianism—

KR: No, Freud won't do. That isn't traditional. That's personal invention. I'm talking about tradition in the strict sense of a revealed spiritual tradition carried by a whole culture, and not theories. The problem is that so much in this world is opinion. I think that Gurdjieff was pretty clear about that. You see, science is inventive, whereas spiritual knowledge is part of revelation, something which is always itself. Experiment belongs to science and material knowledge, but in the last three hundred years, the West has lost track of its traditions because the Christian tradition has become so extremely externalized, and lost its own roots. Most Christians see the world in the scientific mold and add on a sort of cosmetic Christian good will.

AVB: Are the language and symbols of Christianity still useful to us?

KR: All these languages in themselves are totally valid. I would wish to use Christian terms as far as possible, but revitalized through the study of, say, India, or Platonic or Sufi traditions. I think the Catholic Church went badly astray when it adopted Aristotelian philosophy rather than Platonic metaphysics. Aristotelian philosophy ran down into materialist science, dragging the

Christian church along with it. I would like to see an abandonment of Thomist theology and a reconsideration of Christianity in the light of a more spiritual knowledge. Blake was such a Christian, speaking the language of mystics.

AVB: You've spoken of a secret language of poets, of poets taking on the duties of philosophers and churchmen.

KR: When I say poets, I don't mean anyone who writes verse. But, yes, the sacred language has been kept alive by those poets in the underground stream who speak the language of neo-Platonism. You see this in the Renaissance and even in Shakespeare, and of course in the great Romantic revival, which was really a philosophic revival. Coleridge read Plato in the original, and so did Shelley and Wordsworth to a certain extent, whereas Keats and Yeats read the first translation of Plato in English, made by Blake's friend, Thomas Taylor the Platonist. And Blake himself was very much part of the Greek revival which took place at that time; he also knew the Christian esoteric tradition, and Jacob Boehme. And Keats's adage, "Truth is beauty," comes from Plotinus.

But there's never smoke without fire. You can't ask poets to renew culture just off the top of their heads, because they themselves must be the carriers of true knowledge. To look for the revival of culture through the arts is futile, unless the arts themselves are renewed.

When I was young, Eliot was thought to be a wonderful philosophical poet. Eliot was, in his way, quite important as a part of the exoteric Christian tradition. But the poet of the future was really Yeats. Yeats was saying there was going to be a reversal of the gyres, that this was a new age and a crisis of civilization. Now it's very obvious. Scientists themselves have reached the realization that naïve materialism is just not on. The idea that solid matter is somewhere outside of consciousness is no longer scientifically tenable. Nevertheless, the establishment goes on. The universities don't want this; they try to cut everyone down to their own measure. But there's a very vital countermovement now. We're on the attack; we're not on the defensive; we're the new influx coming into the world.

KK: Does it take a great deal of education to participate in this renewal? What about people who can't read?

KR: Literacy and culture are not the same thing. Look at the works of art we study with such passion in the West. Chartres was built by people who couldn't read or write. There are a thousand ways in which tradition can be communicated—in sacred stories, and images, and mythologies. Language at the present time is in the hands of very ignorant people.

I've known some very wise, traditional cultures in Scotland. Unfortunately, in the United States a primitive people hardly exists—though you do have a great indigenous culture that many Americans are looking at rather carefully. I think it is a great pity that the grassroots of Western society are so terribly cut off. Because in traditional societies, the grassroots are very well nourished and they are the nourishment for the more learned levels.

I've just been in India; and while the sun is setting on India and it will all be destroyed in fifty years, *there* is a pre-industrial society. And it's marvelous, because the people live by certain values, they live from a sense of the sacred. And they have marvelous crafts—the things they wear, the way they build their houses—the whole of their culture is there at a very simple level. I saw a wonderful puppet show in the villages; the narration was done by an old, old woman in a tattered sari; she sat on the ground and recited the *Ramayana*.

In America, you have the Native Americans, and the Blacks, and jazz— that is perhaps your greatest living tradition. But otherwise, your grassroots are receptacles for the worst of commercialism, television, and all the rubbish.

AVB: It's certainly true that gospel singing has kept the language of the Gospels alive.

KR: Yes, absolutely. The language has to be kept alive at both ends—by scholars, philosophers, and great artists, and at the simple level also. I hope it can begin to permeate again those alienated areas that are furthest from their true roots. Look at the number of people who can't bear their lives and go to psychiatrists. Meaning can be communicated from within—this is an important concept. But that's been confused by the psychiatric profession.

AVB: I enjoyed the anecdote in your autobiography about your friend whose psychiatrist said, "I can't help you." And your friend said, "Pray for me, then." And the psychiatrist said, "We don't believe in prayer."

KR: Yes, I know, that was true!

AVB: Who, then, are the guardians of language, other than poets, of course, who care so much about language?

KR: I don't think a poet as such is a guardian of language. Poets are guardians of language only when they are guarding tradition. Others who are guardians are the philosophers, insofar as they are using words as the medium for communicating true knowledge. But linguistic philosophers like Ayer—they're not guardians of knowledge. Really, anyone who uses words in order to communicate true knowledge is a guardian of language. Whereas anyone who is using words which once had spiritual content in a reductionist manner is emptying words.

You see, you can either fill words with meaning or you can empty meaning out of words. We're living in a linguistically reductionist society. Everything means less and less. But words can be retrieved and reused so that meaning is put back into them.

I had a letter from the poet Robert Duncan, who wrote a sequence of poems, "Meditations on Rumi." He said that for years he had been reading Rumi in different translations and the words remained pretty meaningless. And then he had a very painful personal experience and something said: Go back to Rumi. And he said the words were absolutely on fire. In Arberry's words, he could hear Rumi's voice. And he said that as he read Rumi, his own answering poem came to him, as if he were talking to Rumi.

It's very interesting that the words were meaningless. Because words in themselves have no meaning. It's only the necessary experience that fills the words. Many people read poems which assume a certain experience, and the words are meaningless to them. But if they have even a little of that illumination, then the words will relive. You can read the Bible and it means nothing. Or, suddenly, given some personal experience, you read the same words and the tears flow to your eyes!

AVB: Do you have a theory about the origin of language? Was it to sing or to pray or to say: "Pass the fire, please?"

KR: Oh, no. I haven't any views at all about that! But I do think man was a spiritual being from the very beginning. I don't think language was meant only for material things. I think that language had many meanings from the beginning, as in the Jewish scriptures, where they say there are four meanings for every text: it has its historic meaning, its psychological meaning, its analogical meaning, and so on. This idea that there are different levels of meaning is the traditional one. The idea that words only mean a fact is a diminution of the normal. The normal, you see, is complete. In early use of language, I imagine, if you named a tree you weren't just naming a species you were going to cut down. Language had an innately sacred dimension. Insofar as it named something, it was naming something that had an existence in all four worlds. But I'm speculating. I'm not a linguistic philosopher.

AVB: But what about revelation through speech? Words come to us, we are inspired, we hear certain phrases. Surely you have this experience in the making of a poem.

KR: Christ was called the Word in the sense of being the medium—in the sense that meaning precedes articulation. That is what I've been trying to say, really. Articulation and the imitation of articulation, which is common speech, isn't really communicating meaning. It is meaning that is primary. But Christ is the Word in the symbolic sense because the Word is all created beings, because nature is a great utterance, because everything in nature is entrusted with meaning from the highest level of creation. We've lost that sense: that we cannot have, as it were, a physical sensation without its also being a communication of knowledge. This is what is so wrong with materialist thought. We say things, but they haven't meaning. They only have the properties of existence, which, if you like, is the very lowest form of meaning.

In its purity, creation is totally meaningful and in that sense imbued with the Word, because the whole creation exists in the manifestation of Christ. The Father is unknowable but Christ is knowable. But I'm guessing. I'm only trying to answer questions that can't really be answered.

AVB: Your poems make a great use of nature and natural imagery. You use vocabulary, it seems, in which even a stone is a word.

KR: Oh yes, that is quite true. From my peasant childhood until now, this is one of the things which has not only stayed with me, but renewed itself—the meaningfulness of nature. It is a book: the book of nature. There are two Words of revelation: one through the Scriptures, and the other in nature.

I know that urban, industrialized, computerized man utterly exposed to television and the movies is about as cut off from this as anyone can be. We indoctrinate the whole society with materialism; the West and the Communist countries are equally brainwashed into this way of seeing the universe; it's soul-destroying.

KK: There are words which are negative and destructive and very, very strong.

KR: Yes, there are. All the time, there are words of, so to speak, anti-power, which reduce or destroy the capacity to experience.

KK: Sometimes people hear words and latch onto them, thinking they understand the meaning. Even the word "holy."

KR: All the words in the present climate of thought have been emptied. There are no words which will hold their meaning in the absence of that meaning. So it's the meanings that have to be rediscovered, and then the words will be refilled.

AVB: It's what we bring to words, and where they come from in us.

KR: It is. Spoken from a cynical, commercial point of view, words mean nothing. You see, commercialism takes everything that is sacred and destroys it immediately. It becomes kitsch. Kitsch is anything which can be bought and sold.

AVB: You have written on Coleridge's definition of the symbol. How does that pertain to sacred language? What is a symbol?

KR: Difficult questions! A symbol presumes the existence of different levels. A symbol isn't using a part as representative of the whole. A symbol presumes that everything that is known by our senses has a corresponding meaning in other levels of experience. The symbol is the natural object, whatever it may be, which will communicate the other levels of the language. There are two kinds of symbols: there are natural symbols, where the meaning is contained in the thing itself, and there are cultural symbols. For example, the cross, for a Christian, immediately means something other than itself. It resonates at every level, through the whole of our being, not just our senses. It's partly a cultural thing, and partly in nature itself.

I don't know if PARABOLA has gotten around to Gaston Bachelard. He was a phenomenologist who tried to purify the language of science of such figurative phrases as "acids *attacking* a base" or "iron magnets *attracting* filings." He said these were anthropomorphic concepts. He found himself at home in the symbolist tradition and he wrote books on the four elements, on water and air, earth and fire. And he said that each of these elements reflects us; the match is absolute. Still water corresponds to a certain mood in us. The ascent of the skylark is the ascent of the spirit.

Nature hands you this marvelous vocabulary every day! And we don't hear it. But primitive people are very sensitive to the language of nature; they notice, for example, the omens of birds.

In my own poetry, I try to use these very simple words of nature, which don't have a lot of recondite associations. To read Yeats, you need to know the sounding board of our whole culture, you need to know about Pythagoras and Hamlet and Phydias, because Yeats touches these strings. But Blake writes:

> To see a World in a Grain of Sand
> And a Heaven in a Wild Flower
> Hold Infinity in the palm of your hand
> And Eternity in an hour

Anyone can understand that.

If She's Not Gone, She Lives There Still

P. L. Travers and Michael Dames

From PARABOLA Vol. 3, No. 1, "Sacred Space"

Michael Dames is the author of **The Silbury Treasure** and **The Avebury Cycle** (both Thames & Hudson), which express his controversial theories about two of Britain's most famous megalithic sites.

P. L. Travers, a consulting editor to PARABOLA from its inception, was the author of many books and essays. Her works include **What the Bee Knows** (Arkana), **About the Sleeping Beauty** (McGraw-Hill), and the Mary Poppins books.

P. L. TRAVERS: I have always been deeply interested in stone circles, and I've just come back from Rollwright, from a modern Druid ceremony for All Soul's Day, which of course is the Druids' ancient New Year. The ceremony itself was hilarious: the Druids, male and female, dressed up like Scott of the Antarctic (it was bitterly cold) with their Druid cloaks over their furs, cavorting about among the stones and handing each other hardboiled eggs. But the stones themselves! They were marvelous, magic, charged with power, ancient and serene, taking no notice of anybody. I longed to be left alone with them, to stay with them till sunset when, so the local people say, they go down to the river to bathe. Once, at Chartres, left alone by a party of friends who wanted to look at the crypt, I just sat there in the great silence feeling something—I still can't give it a name—gathering about me and the top of my head slowly rising. Something is going to be told me, I thought. And then the group came rushing back and my moment was gone forever. When I told an archaeologist friend about this he said, "No wonder. Don't you know of the old legend that under the cathedral is a Neolithic stone circle? That's why they built it there." And I remember seeing Stonehenge, misty in the moonlight, and having something of the same feeling. A thirteen-year-old boy whom I was driving to his new public school (what in America would be a private school) stood beside me, and I wondered if it seemed to him, too, that the stones were lifting into the air, dancing, one could almost say. He was silent, but as we turned back to the car, he said, "After that, I could stand anything. That circle makes one feel protected." Now does all this, in your mind, refer to Avebury and Silbury? I feel quite sure it must.

MICHAEL DAMES: Yes; and I think your remarks about the slightly unsatisfactory quality of the Druid takeover of the Rollwrights refer to what was for me the starting point.

The digging into the largest prehistoric man-made mountain in Europe, which is Silbury Hill in North Wiltshire, was begun on the basis that it contained a patriarchal burial of a prince, a ruler from the Bronze or Iron Age; and it wasn't until 1968, the last of many such digs, that conclusive proof came that in fact the monument was Stone Age or Neolithic, and so for that matter, as had been proved slightly earlier, was the adjacent stone circle, perhaps the greatest in the world, of Avebury. So what we're dealing with there is a group of monuments, within sight of each other, which by common consent formed the metropolis of Neolithic Britain. The first, and I would say possibly the greatest, British civilization was unquestionably based on the cult of the Great Goddess. Now, once the date was known, archaeologists asserted they would be able to link those tremendous physical remains to an accepted body of belief and a culture; but conspicuously this hasn't been done yet. I would say a conspiracy of silence has descended; so that about 1970, living in the area, I was overwhelmed by this sense of discontinuity, really, between the archaeologists' avowed intent to make cultural sense of what they'd found and what actually happened—which was *nothing,* in the way of interpretation. So I began to try to find out as much as I could about Neolithic culture, having had an archaeological training in the first place, but being vastly ignorant, as most students of archaeology are, about comparative religion, folklore, and ethnographic

Stone Age communities. We just never come across the material in a conventional archaeological course.

PLT: That's what one misses in all archaeology. It demands the proof, but it doesn't care about the meaning.

MD: Well, I'm not against careful collection of data, but ultimately one has to have the modesty to carry that data to a point of view, a way of looking at it that is different from the narrowly rational—a point of view where symbolism in all its richness becomes rational. Now one of the things that struck me about Silbury was that all the effort had gone into concentrating on this vast conical mound with the flat top, and no effort at all had been directed toward the surrounding moat, which is 1100 feet long and curiously curved in a way that doesn't make any kind of engineering sense. But this great "quarry," if you like, fills up with water (even though there's fifteen feet of silt in the ditch now) regularly once a year. It occurred to me that what one was looking at there was a monument which was also an image, an image of the Great Mother whose body was defined by this lake, and whose belly, or full womb, was the mound; so that the Harvest Mother, pregnant, was there lying on the ground as a picture. And not only a picture, but a picture that *moved,* with the help of sunlight and moonlight; the reflected strength of the two eyes in the sky comes to the Mother and helps her completion. By saying that I wish to indicate two things: first of all, the long axis of her reclining body is bang on an east-west line, that marvelous spindle of equilibrium between the seasons where night and day are of equal duration. And then if you go there at the quarter day, Lammas, the traditional start of harvest in Britain, you'll see the moon coming up over an adjacent spring and striking its first light on her water thigh at exactly the place where you expect a child's head to emerge. Then as the night goes on, this flicker of moonlight moves around the Mother, onto her knee, and crosses a narrow natural causeway of undisturbed chalk before filling up progressively a "child" moat, a little disconnected piece of moat which is hugged tight against the belly mound of the hill itself; and the moon goes on through the night and eventually sets on the breast, so that the last moonlight you see is a flicker of white on the breast. I regard this as an intentional, *kinetic* representation of the harvest birth. The child isn't born to starve, but to drink; and simultaneously on the hundred feet of flat summit there's a little cornfield with room for the first fruits festival to take place.

PLT: Doesn't that refer to the old idea that "she"—I call her "she" because I feel very strongly with you that whatever this is, it is a maternal symbol—that the mound was constructed "while a posset of milk was seething"?

MD: Yes, that's fascinating. The folklore fragment which you quote was recorded by John Aubrey in the mid-seventeenth century, and seems completely random and meaningless—that a hill was built while a posset was seething; but it really fits in precisely. What is the posset? It is the underworld, if you like, the world beneath the lake, the world trapped in the rock; and at harvest, with the coming of the right moment, the milk swirls up and creates a mound of joyful food, a sacred liquid. And of course the cult of the corn dolly, which now fills our gift shops, once filled the reality of farming with imagery which went on from the harvest back into the farmhouse and the barn in winter, and then was returned to the field to be ploughed in the following spring, creating a great cycle, which I think the adjacent monuments helped to celebrate.

But you were asking me, before we started taping, about the name Silbury, weren't you?

PLT: Yes. You say in your book that first of all they thought that there was buried there some mythological figure called King Sil.

MD: Yes, that's right. There are two ways of looking at the King Sil fragment. One can think of it as a later patriarchal injection which developed as time went on, because King Sil was transformed in the eighteenth century into a golden monarch on a horse, full-sized.

PLT: Transformed in the mind of the folk, you mean.

MD: Yes, but I think there's also a possibility, at least, of an original theme there, insofar as the goddess worldwide always has a male consort, and if he's a consort of corn, he's golden. So I haven't quite made my mind up about which of those to choose!

PLT: I would accept that; it's a good mythological analogy, and perhaps that was in the folk. When I say "the folk," you know, I mean naturally the people of that time, who lived in fields and hills; but, for that matter, we're all "folk"—the people who walk in the streets. We forget it; we despise the term. But really we ourselves are the folk and quite capable of absorbing this mythological material when given to us.

MD: I think that's very important indeed. We're not really dealing with history, something chronologically remote, but with that eternal present that real myth deals with. Certainly my working on Silbury has helped me to endure living in the city, rather than the opposite; because all forms of earthly bounty are basically holy whether they come in cans or carts. But one of the things that interests me particularly about the Wiltshire monuments around Silbury is their unique relationship to the natural land forms. In central Wiltshire the downs undulate in a marvelously anthropomorphic manner, and it does rather seem like an extended body going on mile after mile. Indeed, the Wiltshire place-names emphasize that that was how the "folk" viewed their countryside. Now when we're asked why did they choose the particular locality of Avebury to make this supreme effort, I think the answer lies in two springs which are very close by: Swallowhead and the adjacent Waden Spring. These two springs happen by a stupendous geographical fluke to line up with the Lammas quarter day sunrise, 70° east and north in one direction, and the Lammas moonset at 250° east and north in the other. So that presented with this "cue" by the goddess landscape, they responded with the supreme statement of this architectural image very close by. It is an interesting fact that water from Swallowhead Spring was taken to the top of Silbury and drunk on Mothering Sunday* as late as 1850.

PLT: You know, that brings us right back to a study I recently made of the nursery rhyme, "Jack and Jill." Pondering upon this, I thought, why would they go *up* the hill? Water notoriously flows down to the lowest place. Then I discovered a clue in Sweden. Jack and Jill were supposed to have been seen by Mani, the moon, going up the hill to take water from the sacred well of Brigir. So they were taken up and put in the moon, and the Swedes think that, where we see a man in the moon, they see Jack and Jill carrying the water. And you say in your book that even quite lately, perhaps a hundred years ago, people were carrying fresh spring water up to the top of Silbury to drink it there ceremonially and religiously. Don't you think it refers?

MD: Absolutely. Isn't that amazing? Yes, I think there's a strong possibility of that.

How to get on into the next season I suppose is the problem that farmers worry about; although it happens inevitably. I don't know whether you would agree that the basic myth of the world seems to be to bring people to the next threshold with a sense of its rightness and its appropriateness in time, rather than to have any kind of jerkiness or trauma about the change. It's very interesting to me, having spent so long working on Silbury, that from the top you

*The fourth Sunday in Lent, when motherhood and the Mother of the Gods were especially honored.

can see this marvelous long barrow, which is 330 feet long, on the adjoining down—the West Kennet long barrow—and if one accepts the credibility of architecture-as-image (and certainly people like Philip Rawson and Vincent Scully and Joseph Campbell would seem to accept that), then what is this long thing? Well, I suggest in my latest book, *The Avebury Cycle,* that we're looking there at the "Hag"—or I think your word was "Crone"—and the crone with its long spine of sandstone boulders, covered with chalk, has a hollow end to it; in this case, the funeral chambers of West Kennet long barrow. The chambers are five-lobed; and they are a dreadful place. They were visited well over a thousand years, as archaeologists have proved, and the population wandered amongst the rotting remains of jumbled-up corpses; a terrible, terrible spectacle. And yet isn't this just the way to wisdom that in certain Tantric traditions is known to be both necessary and, in the end, loving?

PLT: Indeed, in the Tantric scripture the Great Mother represents this, too. And when you talk about the long barrows, aren't you telling also of those you can find in Ireland? I have been in the Brugh of Angus, which is now called New Grange. They have made it a place fit for tourists now, with electric light, and enlarged the opening so that people can stand up and walk through into the sacred inner chamber. But in the old days, I remember having to crawl through that narrow birth-passage, if you like, or otherwise death-passage, on my hands and knees, with a candle. And in the central chamber—I don't know whether you've seen it—it's all carved and marked with the most mysterious hieroglyphs. I was alone in there with the man who had persuaded me to this awful adventure. And I was overcome with the vibrations and the sense of power that was in this place. I could hardly stand it. It was very like, but much greater than, what I felt at Chartres. One was overcome by these tremendous—oh, sensations isn't the right word! One's whole body was vivified; it was almost unbearable.

MD: That's interesting: the comparison you bring up with New Grange as it's now called, in that the long tunnel there, landing up in this cruciform chamber, seems as you say like being born in reverse—being born to the underworld. And that's why I find the shape of the West Kennet long barrow funeral chambers absolutely fascinating, because they seem to be an enlarged version of the squatting goddess image, which is usually connected with birth—many authorities regard the Neolithic figurines as portrayals of the act of parturition—only now in her deathly aspect, hidden within this long barrow mound. Here is the squatting goddess as receiver into the world of chaos, into the world of the collapse of vegetable form, into the world of ploughing and winter. Round the chambers runs a river of dry stonewallings, which have been carried there from thirty miles away, which I think simulate the dry river which the Old Hag of Scottish folklore is said to have created at the winter quarter day, at Martinmas; with her skinny arm and thin wand she touched the rivers and they turned to stone. And here one sees such a river as part of the architecture.

I suppose at this time of year—here we are sitting in the darkest part of the year—one always longs for spring. One of the big questions about the Avebury Cycle is how did they effect this wonderful miracle of springtime? My scrutiny of the evidence seems to suggest that it was effected with great difficulty and concentrated effort. Many primitive communities divide their adolescents, boys from girls, and the boys and girls both and separately die to childhood and are born as adults.

PLT: I'd like to know this—did they have, in your thinking, a rite of passage by which they made the transit from childhood to adolescence, to maturity? Have we any evidence of this?

MD: Well, I think the archaeological hardware is there. In the case of the female incarceration at the onset of puberty, there is a temple called the Sanctuary ideally suited to such a function. It was a conical hut built of wood, sixty-five feet in diameter—that incidentally is the distance from Swallowhead Spring to the main river, and it's also the diameter of a wattle ring buried in the very core of Silbury. So standing in the doorway of the Sanctuary hut, an adolescent girl was standing in the hollow form of the kernel of Silbury in a hut which archaeologists reconstruct in exactly the same shape as Silbury itself, only of course much smaller; and she could see her maternal future silhouetted against the skyline in the shape of the chalk mound which overlaid the wattle bands at the core of Silbury.

PLT: Would you say (I know we only speak mythologically) that Avebury with its long avenues and its great circle of stones and its inner sanctuaries of sun and moon, stands in relation to Silbury as maiden stands to mother?

MD: I think that is quite likely, with the slight qualification that it is Maiden and her Bridegroom in relation to Mother. If we got as far as the Sanctuary for the girls, the stone avenue called the West Kennet avenue leads from there to the Avebury Henge, and an equivalent avenue called the Beckhampton leads to the same Avebury Henge: this massive ditch and ring of standing stones, some of them over fourteen feet high, within which there are two circles. Now

I think of the Avebury Henge as a wedding ring, both in the human sense and also the marriage of cattle, and also the wedding of the binary opposites of yin and yang coming together to make the start of a new generation of happenings. In saying that, I hope to establish what is well known in every other part of the world where Neolithic culture has been studied: namely, that the synchronization of the farming year—the activity of ploughing the soil and seeding it and watching the crop rise and eventually harvesting it—is synchronized, I believe, in imagery, with stages in the human life cycle. When we get to the Henge, we get to coitus, to the lovematch; and the shape of the outer bank, which again, like Silbury, is water-filled—that's why they dug down so far; it's now silt-filled—the shape I believe is based on that U-shape that you can see on the goddess' apron in Minoan Crete; you can see it in India and certainly you can see it in Swallowhead Spring. That design is equivalent to the human female vulva from which all waters flow. Now the male avenue, Beckhampton Avenue, is extended into that female containing-shape in a feature known as the D feature: a setting of stones within one of the two internal circles. So that architecturally again, the marriage, the serpentine energy of spring—in the Celtic tradition, the maiden was the serpent—these serpentine energies meet and coalesce at Avebury. And from Avebury, if you stand at the center of that great temple, you can just see the summit of Silbury hill over the horizon.

PLT: You see what's in store for you, in fact! You see what's waiting.

MD: Exactly. That's right. Before literacy, you may manifest that which you desired in art and architecture. And architecture is the mother of the arts; it contains the smaller icons; it is the platform for human performance. And it is an astounding grief to me that we've deprived ourselves of this knowledge of architecture as a symbolic imagery and are content with mere building. What a deprivation to inflict upon oneself willingly! I don't understand it. About two years after I had begun my exploration into the meaning of the monuments, I had the great good fortune to come across Cassirer's great book, *The Philosophy of Symbolic Forms,* and with delight I realized that the principles of mythic space awareness which he elucidated there completely confirmed my gradually accumulating convictions concerning the nature of sacred space in and between the Wiltshire monuments. In particular, his statement that "the development of the mythical feeling of space always starts from the opposition of day and night, light and darkness," fitted exactly my feelings about the primary natural symbol in the area, the Swallowhead Spring. There, the black hole in the white chalk rock is the unforgettable doorway between two worlds, inviting movement in both directions. In fact, the annual fluctuation in the water table yearly enacts this interplay—the stream sinking back into the ground in autumn, and spouting forth anew in early spring. In the Silbury and Avebury monuments, the movement between dark and light also has an aquatic aspect. Flights of Neolithic steps carved out with antler tines lead from below the water level in the deeply quarried moats at the Silbury water breast, and at the marriage henge. Walking through the surface of the magic water mirror, the population could enter the dark liquid body of the Lady of the Lake, and emerge with an intuitive and factually correct understanding of the source of all life. Equally, one is led to realize that far from being an arbitrary choice, the preference for an east-west axis in monument planning is another consequence of the light-dark structure of the year at the gateway between winter and summer, marking sunrise and sunset positions at the equinoxes, the perfect equilibrium. Similarly, the light climax of each day and of every full-moon night registers due south when those bodies are highest in the sky. Is it no more than an accident that the bridegroom's door to the Avebury Henge, and the vulva of the Silbury birth goddess, *and* the sacred Swallowhead Spring, *and* sun and moon at zenith, are in alignment, due north-south?

PLT: All you're saying leads me to think of the extraordinarily natural order in the way of life of these Neolithic people. They followed the laws of sun and moon and seasons and in that way they must have served their goddess, served her faithfully—because wasn't she their mother? And faithfully she gave them increase. Now look what's happened to us: the goddess has become the state. Nobody shows it any duty or service; everybody says "I want, I want," and expects to be freely given to, as once the Mother gave— but in return for service.

MD: Yes. I think one thing that follows from what you've just said is the way we tend nowadays to separate the cerebral from the physical, which I suppose is the legacy of Christianity, that activity of division; whereas in what one can discover of the pattern of life in Neolithic communities, there's no such separation. What confirmation can we find of this merging of physical and intellectual at the Avebury monuments? I think one can see them as double images, quite legitimately. I've spoken of the Avebury horseshoe as a vulva with phallus incorporated into it. But it is equally possible to see it as "skull" with two inner circles as eye sockets or eyes. Similarly if you look at Silbury itself from the east, it's the squatting Mother with the moat. If you look at it from the west, it's a huge eyeball in a water head, so that the division between spirit and body which we've suffered from for the last two thousand years seems never to have been an issue there at all. And the iconography supports this total fusion of those two aspects of human existence.

PLT: The sense of sacredness must have been within them, not only in the shape of the earth, their tellurian temple. This reminds me of something that was written in the early seventeenth century by a writer named Samuel Purchas, in his book *Microcosmos*. He says, "Why then, O man, know thyself and know all things. Thou hast thy body, a book of nature, and carriest a little model of the greater world continually about thee." Wasn't this what Avebury and Silbury were telling us, that in a sense, we're in the Great Mother; and alternately, the Great Mother is in us. We can't escape.

MD: Yes; and I'm convinced (with Lévi-Strauss and Cassirer) that the Neolithic peoples knew that, and brought the physical reality of the body into their architecture as a mode of measurement. In Avebury parish I find that they sought to construct their buildings using a linear module derived from a fusion of the two aspects of physical reality uppermost in their experience—namely the human body, and the external environment understood as a superhuman body. I believe that this fusion was effected by that most physical of measuring devices, the human stride. Plainly they strode everywhere, but in seeking a sacred module as the basis of an architecture whose function was to heighten the sacredness of the local natural endowment, they might be expected to turn to the landscape at its most potently active—that is, to the two springs of Swallowhead and Waden, and to pace out the trickle of waters from chalk source to the river Kennet. These tributaries, the lifeways of the Goddess-landscape running so memorably from the underworld, were regarded as sacred till the eighteenth century. Today these tributaries, measured in abstract (yet sensuously derived) feet are sixty-five feet and four hundred feet respectively. Is it just coincidence that both these modules occur over and over again in the major dimensions of all the Avebury monuments? For example, sixty-five feet is the diameter of Silbury core fence, the diameter of the Sanctuary hut, the width of the West Kennet long barrow facade, and the distance between the Avebury circles. The Silbury mound height is sixty-five feet by two feet, and dozens of examples of simple multiples appear to be present throughout the ensemble.

The validity of turning to the springs for measuring rods would have been greatly enhanced for them by reason of their alignment on the sunrise-moonset quarter day axis, 70°–250° east of north; and the local building module would have received some of its authority from the celestial hemisphere and some from the underworld, at critical moments in the annual cycle of each.

Since the buildings themselves were each designed to engage in a dialogue between Above and Below, balanced about the soil line (the farmers' equator), the rationale of a measured loyalty to the *genius loci* becomes strong. In particular contrast to our own abstract numerology, the plotting of Neolithic sacred space depends, I believe, on populating the landscape with figures, *human* figures, prepared to walk the superhuman geography, and to extend what was found into an architecture loyal to the place of its foundation. The awareness of space, and measured space as *active* rather than static, is also brought into focus by the two lengths of running water, whose vitality was subsequently embodied in, and reflected by, the kinetic, living architecture, as a genetic inheritance.

Around the four great monuments we've been discussing, there is an even larger image of the Great Mother, I believe, composed of twenty-six long barrows and certain other circles and causeway camps, which occupies a twenty-five-square-mile tract of downland, and all these are Neolithic sites. They have their arms, or horns if you like, along the crests of the downs, overlooking the Vale of Pewsey, and from there the whole majestic figure can be seen stretching away into the distance. In their very core, in their gut, are the monuments: Silbury, West Kennet long barrow, the avenues of the Avebury Henge, as almost internal tracts to this larger image—although each of the internal monuments operates as an image in its own right. So as you say, it goes from the very smallest individual to the very largest thing imaginable, the universe. And all intermediate stages were accessible to these people, because they had this basic micro-macro view of things, which we talk about rather glibly perhaps nowadays without allowing for the physical outcome of that idea in the view of primitive society: namely, that that whole territory, that whole country was a figure, a body. One can hear the peoples in the Sudan today speaking of the marsh areas of their lands as the Mother's groin and the upland mountains as her breasts. The key to primitive geography of the world can be seen in such a group of monuments as we have there.

The other thing is in the sense of space: all of these things laid out in space; I think it's wrong to isolate space from time. Sacred space, I believe, is a marriage of space with time. And the space becomes sacred at certain prescribed times, and then becomes prosaic again until the next bringing together of space and time. The word "Silbury" itself comes from the Old English "blessed time," "harvest time"—so the Silbury moat lights up for the birth moment at that blessed time.

I think that's what I feel about sacred space in that particular area.

PLT: The poet and sage A. E. used to say to me when I was very young, "The earth is a living being." You're actually saying that this is what the people of the Neolithic times thought, not only of their temples, but of their planet.

MD: Exactly. Yes, they needed the temples to confirm and bring into sharper focus that which they believed already about the world in general. For that reason, people came from all over the British Isles to the Avebury Cycle of monuments, as has been shown by archaeological finds. It was truly a national focus for eternity, the year rolling on as a great circle of interlocking events. Indeed it was still being used in Saxon and medieval times, so that it had an enormously long life-span, as is right for a farming cycle attached to the Great Goddess who seems able to skip with ease across racial divisions and political upheavals.

PLT: Oh, she does! She is mentioned in Taoist texts as the Mountain Mother. There's your Silbury again. In Japan, she's a peach tree. The oldest fairy tale in Japan is called "Peach Boy" and he's born of this peach tree. In China, the symbol for the Great Mother is jade. It's the symbol at once of death and immortality. You find her everywhere. You can't take a step without her! In my field, which I think of as the fairy tale, you can always tell the antiquity of a tale when it has, as its chief character, a woman. She always refers to the Great Mother. For instance, in "Snow White," "Cinderella," "Allerleirauh," and above all "The Sleeping Beauty."

MD: This is marvelous, because the fragments of the tattered remains of the English folk tradition are really little episodes in this great story, the only central story from which all other stories derive—that of the seasonal metamorphosis of the central divine being and her male consort.

PLT: We see it in one of the oldest English anonymous poems:

> *I sing of a maiden who is mateless,*
> *King of all kings, her son she chose.*

She chose—which means, in essence, she accepted—accepted in every sense. He's clearly lover as well as son.

MD: Yes. Even in post-medieval times there has been, up until the Puritan revolution, a capacity for the Great Mother to survive in amongst, and infuse a certain kind of life into, Christianity on the one hand and the most uninformed folk appetites on the other. There is a wonderful value there.

I think if one looks for a folk image to set alongside the two stone avenues going to the Avebury Wedding Ring, one can't do better than go to a village in Staffordshire called Abbots Bromley, where dancers including Maid Marian and Dirty Bet go around and beat the bounds of the parish and form two snaky dances which lead into a circle—two serpents coalescing in a circle. It seems to be a very important theme in folk dancing. It's certainly true there, and the horned aspect of the goddess is also part of that rite because most of the dancers carry huge stag horns or reindeer horns.

PLT: Isn't it so that these dances—I've seen them myself—are all performed with the utmost gravity, as though they were a service to something that perhaps the dancers have forgotten?

MD: Yes, there's a stateliness about them.

PLT: Wouldn't you say that perhaps all dance, however profane, is, even if unconsciously, done before the Lord? Remember in the Apocryphal Book of St. John, in the Hymn of Jesus where he makes the disciples stand about him in a ring. They dance and sing—strophe and antistrophe.

MD: Yes, because what is dance? It is the kinetic involvement of the individuals in a thing greater than themselves, a pattern which can turn from solar orb into serpentine river-flow with an ordered measure to it, the bringing of order into the random chaos of overwhelming experience. I know from having camped in a thunderstorm near Silbury that one can be scared out of one's wits by the alarming power of natural forces even in the mild and melodious southern English countryside.

At all times the community has sought to order this in an affirmative way and to face the terrors of existence, and to come to terms with them.

PLT: Do you think that these ideas that have grown up in you around Silbury and Avebury are still available to the folk? Are there any legends connected with Avebury and Silbury, such as there are with the Rollwright stones who go down to the river to bathe and to drink? What do the people round about think? Is she still the holy place?

MD: No, in the organized sense of Mother Goddess worship—I don't think there's any such activity; but in the broader sense, the Neolithic realities, what were they? Moving clouds, rain, sunshine—things coming out of the ground, things dying into the ground. Those are our realities. We still eat food from the ground—it comes from nowhere else.

PLT: Though for us, it comes from the supermarket.

MD: Ah, but the supermarket is the ground, except it's moved sideways slightly! Similarly, the movements of the population to the coasts at Lammas, the great July-August rush. I can't bring myself to despise the seaside paraphernalia because if we despise our sun at our seaside, then we have no right to speak joyfully of the Neolithic, because the physical realities still potentially contain as much sacredness as they ever did.

PLT: Well—perhaps it's not so much that she is lost to us, but (aside from the sense in which you're speaking) we are in a way lost to her, except insofar as a handful of us remember our service to her. There is said to be the remnants of a Celtic tribe still living in the wilds of Derbyshire where life is lived according to the laws of the Great Mother. She's worshipped there. I heard about it and I promised I wouldn't try to track them down, though I would very much like to talk to them. Perhaps it's true that like the seasons, all things come around again; I think it is true. There's an old nursery rhyme that you yourself quoted in *The Silbury Treasure:*

> *There was an old woman lived under a hill,*
> *And if she's not gone, she lives there still.*

MD: Yes. And I think that for everyone born of woman, the relationship between the individual and the containing maternal shape is so fundamental during our first nine months of pre-life that it is impossible to eradicate it from any group of adults in a complete and decisive and final way. It represents, even in its submerged state, a form of reality which attaches us both to our literal mothers and to the earth in general.

PLT: So, at Silbury, she lives there still.

MD: Right!

Finding Our Place

Belonging

THOMAS BERRY

Vol. 24, No. 1
"Nature"

The Risk of
Evolution

JOSEPH CHILTON
PEARCE

Vol. 17, No. 2
"Labyrinth"

The Nature of
Consciousness

OLIVER SACKS

Vol. 22, No. 3
"Conscience and
Consciousness"

Belonging

An Interview with Thomas Berry

From PARABOLA Vol. 24, No. 1, "Nature"

Thomas Berry is a cultural historian and scholar of world religions. His books include **The Universe Story** with Brian Swimme (HarperSanFrancisco) and **The Great Work** (Bell Tower).

Nancy Stetson and **Penny Morrell** developed much of this interview material in the course of filming a documentary on Berry's thought.

PARABOLA: Does our relation to nature connect with our inner human development?

THOMAS BERRY: The outer world is necessary for the inner world; they're not two worlds but a single world with two aspects: the outer and the inner. If we don't have certain outer experiences, we don't have certain inner experiences, or at least we don't have them in a profound way. We need the sun, the moon, the stars, the rivers, and the mountains and the trees, the flowers, the birds, the song of the birds, the fish in the sea, to evoke a world of mystery, to evoke the sacred. It gives us a sense of awe. This is a response to the cosmic liturgy, since the universe itself is a sacred liturgy. Humans become religious by joining the religion of the universe. Apart from that, our souls shrivel and our imagination is dulled. If we lived on the moon, our imagination would be as flat as the moon, our emotions would be dull, and our sense of the divine would reflect the lunar landscape. The experience of the grandeur and beauty of the outer world is totally necessary.

P: What is the meaning of "nature"?

TB: "Nature" comes from *natos,* to be born. It has to do with that dynamic principle that holds something together and gives it its identity. When we speak about the nature of a thing, the nature is most clearly expressed in genetic coding, because the genetic coding contains the pattern that guides the organism in the whole complex of activities that any living organism has to perform. The nature has to do with the form of the thing. For instance, an oak tree is different from a maple tree. It's the nature of the oak to produce acorns, and it's the nature of the maple to produce maple sugar. The word "nature" is also used for the whole complex of the world of the living, generally the nonhuman world of the living. But in reality we are an integral part of what we call nature, the dynamic principle that holds the world of the living together. Nature is an organizing presence, the deepest dimension of the universe. We can understand an ordering principle in a single organism as its genetic coding or pattern. But the pattern that gives order to the whole world of the living—and not only of the living, but also the world of the nonliving—is too mysterious. To describe nature gives order to the universe, what St. Thomas refers to as the ultimate and noblest perfection in things.

P: Do humans play a unique role in the evolution of nature?

TB: Each thing has a unique role in the universe, and its identity gives it value. The difference of things is the value of things; only if one thing is different from another can each give something to the other. If things were the same, nothing could pass between them through which each would gain in its presence to the other. This exists throughout the universe—it takes a whole universe to make each reality. So too with the human. Sometimes people say, "Well, they're all of equal value." But to make everything equal takes away the value of everything. Of the universe itself. St. Thomas says that the whole universe together participates in and manifests the divine more than any single being whatsoever. He also says the order of the universe is the ultimate and noblest perfection in things. Relatively speaking, each thing is the best. When it comes to flying, the birds are the best. When it comes to swimming, the fish are the best. When it comes to reflexive thinking, humans are the best. What is the contribution that the humans make to the universe? We enable the universe to reflect on itself and in a sense to smile at and enjoy itself. While the universe activates itself in each part of the universe, the special attribute of the human is to enable the universe to reflect on itself with a special mode of intelligible self-awareness, to enjoy itself and to celebrate itself in the light of the numinous mystery that is expressed in everything.

P: Is any purpose served in our holding ourselves separate from nature?

TB: There's the temporary gain of self-exaltation and of seeing ourselves over the rest of the universe. The first gain is that it enables the human to exploit the rest of the world, so that there can be economic gain by exalting the human and diminishing the grandeur of the natural world. If you diminish the rights and grandeur of the natural world, then you can exploit it with a lack of restraint until it is turned to a cinder. That's the danger of the path that we're on, because the refuse of the industrial world is so diminished in its inner capacities. The amount of energy is still there, but it has passed from a stage where it can be used to a stage where it cannot be used. The consequences are that we undo the natural world and negate the whole creative process.

P: Is there a mythic basis to a scientific explanation of nature?

TB: Well, I think so. I think our rational processes are involved in mythic expression. For instance, the dynamics of economics are not economic, but are driven by myth or vision or mystique . . . driven by the millennial myth. Western history itself is driven by a mythic commitment to a certain fulfillment, a certain time in history. There will come a thousand years, and then history is to end.

Western civilization is a conflict between the dragon and the woman bearing the child; this is all in the Book of Revelation of St. John (17–22). There the myth of history speaks of a time when the dragon is chained for a thousand years, when there will be peace and plenty and abundance. During this time, humans will transcend the human condition within history. After a thousand years, the dragon will be unchained, and there will be the transcendence of the earthly Jerusalem to the heavenly. This myth is in the background of all Western history. When it was not fulfilled by divine reckoning, we decided to let it speak through science, technology, commerce, and industry. In other words, our whole economics is transrational.

P: Do indigenous peoples retain the knowledge of how to connect to the mythic elements of the natural world?

TB: Indigenous peoples think primarily in mythic expressions. Myth is an analogical way of relating to our surroundings. These stories reflect the human mind's response to the world. Narrative sees the universe as an ongoing drama, romance, or adventure, and so can deal with almost any issues it finds. The human mind in its rational capacities wants everything explained, but sometimes that's not desirable. Something that's been rationalized doesn't have the grandeur or brilliance that you find in mythic forms of expression, and that's why myth is available for everybody. These are the forms that we live by.

P: What is needed to reestablish a reverence for nature?

TB: When people ask me how to reestablish a sense of the sacred, I'm somewhat baffled. It's a primordial experience of being human. When our primordial experiences are dimmed, negated, or impoverished, restoring these abilities is difficult. Yet there's nothing so necessary as a recovery of the sense of the sacred. Catastrophic events sometimes can restore a sense of the awesome, that there are powers greater than the human. This strikes a certain fear, which is why it's sometimes said that fear of the Lord is the beginning of wisdom. An awakening to spiritual powers, something older than physical powers of the universe, is one necessity for developing a sense of reverence.

P: Are you hopeful or not with regard to the future?

TB: I'm constantly asked if I'm hopeful, and it's not an easy question to answer, except that there's no existence without hope. I still work toward a healing of what's wrong, and to create a desirable future. I think constantly of the future—of the children, and of the need for all children to go into the future as a single, sacred community. The children of the trees, the children of the birds, the children of the animals, the children of the insects—all children, including the human children, must go together into the future. There's no future for the human children if there's no future for the children of those other life forms. The vigor and sensitivity of childhood is, for me, one of the great inspirations, because the childhood experience is refreshing, spontaneous, wholehearted, and fearless.

For myself, my sense of meaningful existence has increased rather than decreased, and my sense of hope has certainly increased in the last twenty or thirty years. I was more overwhelmed by the difficulties that we confronted then than I am today. I understand the situation more clearly and can see the greater evils, but I also see a surge of response. There is much more protest now than there was in the 1950s, although the problem is greater. In the 1930s, we made only five hundred thousand tons of industrial chemicals annually. Now, we're making two hundred million tons every year. That makes the whole planet toxic, because these are put to an almost infinite variety of uses. But we have for the first time now the International Society for Ecological Economics—up until ten years ago there was no economics department in the country that would identify human economics as derivative from the earth's economy.

P: I know that you've worked out a story about the origin of nature. I enjoyed your book, cowritten with Brian Swimme, *The Universe Story*. Why is it important to have a story about the origin of the universe?

TB: In its context, we find meaning for our lives—not simply for our personal lives, but lives that are embedded in the universe. Nature is the greater self of every particular being; why else is the scientist so driven to appreciate it? To get a feel for the story of our own lives, we need the story of the universe as the larger, more meaningful context of understanding.

There is a completely new awareness on the part of scientists who have awakened to the fact that their understanding of nature constitutes the epic of our time. A meeting, the Epic of Evolution, was convened under the auspices of the American Association for the Advancement of Science. The astounding thing is to think that we now have an epic that belongs to us. We have invented a new story, one that brings things together and provides meaning. It becomes the myth of our time.

P: My last question is related: Can we look to myth for guidance in our task of healing our nature and the greater nature?

TB: Well, it's the necessary context. I don't know if it's the *only* context, but what we call myth has to do with understanding. All religions find that their deep experience and expression take form in the spirituality of the story, of a deep allegorical form. What we call myth is quintessential for the type of fulfillment a human being needs.

Humans came into being at the end of the planetoid period (that's about sixty-five million years of earth's history), which I call the Lyric period because it was so brilliant. The birds appeared, at their most brilliant, the flowers, the trees, and then the mammals, by form so magnificent. These entities had a very special quality because then humans came into being. Human intelligence requires a magnificent world, a beautiful world, a world of resonance and meaning. For humans to bear the burden of intelligence and responsibility, we need a beautiful world to inspire and heal us.

Myth also is healing. But to lose the natural world is an enormous loss for the whole community. For children not to be able to see the stars or know their stories and have a mythic insight into the stars: it's a soul loss. The greatness of Dante lies in how his poem was structured by the whole cosmology as it was known at that time. It encompassed the whole history of human society as well as all the great historical personages, all the mythic stories of the classical period and the Christian world.

Contact with the natural world goes both ways. Our contact with the natural world evokes the mythic dimension. What's so wrong with our emphasis on rationality is that we close off the mythic world and don't admit it, and the same closing-off of the mythic world closes us off from the natural world, because the natural world is reduced to a use-relationship. A use-relationship with the natural world is the deepest perversity that humans are capable of. The worst thing one human being can say to another is, "You used me." Nature could tell us, "You used me. I'm not here to be used, primarily; I'm here to bestow blessedness, to bestow beauty, to bestow joy and healing, to communicate a sense of the divine. But if you're going to use me . . . I will serve you, I will heal you, I will shelter you, I will feed you, but don't approach me simply from the standpoint of use."

The greatest and deepest tragedy in losing the splendor of the outer world is that we will always have an inner demand for it. We're genetically coded to exist in the world of beauty. Take away the world of beauty, and our genetic coding remains oriented toward that. We will have desires that can never be satisfied. Our integral spiritual development can never take place.

The Risk of Evolution

An Interview with Joseph Chilton Pearce

From PARABOLA Vol. 17, No. 2, "Labyrinth"

Professor and author **Joseph Chilton Pearce** has presented his theories on childhood development and schooling in a number of books, including **The Crack in the Cosmic Egg** (Julian Press), **The Magical Child** (Plume), and **Evolution's End** (HarperSanFrancisco).

PARABOLA: In traditional stories, there's often a treasure at the center of the labyrinth, the forest, the castle of innumerable rooms—and one has to face countless struggles and difficulties, traveling up many blind alleys, to get there, to the heart of things. Isn't human development itself just such a maze or labyrinth, with wrong turns and blind alleys and assorted challenges along the way?

JOSEPH CHILTON PEARCE: Human development is certainly a remarkable maze that opens up or shuts down at various stages of life. At any point there are an infinite number of ways which could be taken. The brain, operating on a high degree of selectivity, determines which way we take, and that shuts off all the other avenues.

There are two periods that we know of in which a major housecleaning takes place in the neurons of the brain. One is right before birth, when certain functional neurostructures that are appropriate only to uterine experience have to be deconstructed, or they would become excess baggage, a hindrance and a block.

Now that is significant on many levels. If we don't develop those structures *in utero* and if that clean-up right before birth doesn't happen, we would be in trouble. Over and over in development there are temporary states, temporary structures, temporary abilities and capacities that unfold. We have to develop these efficiently and completely, and then get out of them. If we don't develop them, or if we get stuck in them and don't move beyond them, there is a breakdown in development, and the self system—our passionate, individual self—can't grow.

The next housecleaning, that takes place at age eleven, is equally complex. If that didn't take place, the child would never be able to socialize or to knuckle down to the great disciplines of mind necessary to move on up into higher intelligence.

But at the same time, due to lack of environmental stimulus and guidance, the average child at this age loses a full eighty percent of all neural connections—and therefore a large percentage of available neural fields.

P: When these connections are lost, doesn't this cause blind alleys in the labyrinth of the brain itself?

JCP: The ability to operate mentally by the process that Piaget called Concrete Operational Thinking can be developed from the age of seven to about eleven. Nature provides a massive neural growth-spurt at about age six to cover this potential, which gives a child's brain some five to seven times the neural capacity of an adult brain. At age eleven other programs in nature's agenda open for exploration and the brain releases a chemical which dissolves all unmyelinated—which means undeveloped or unused—neural fields. She puts the house in order so as to begin a much more restricted but disciplined intellectual journey, which Piaget called Formal Operational Thinking. Those neural structures not used in developing concrete operational thought, foundational to formal thought, would now get in the way, clutter up the operations, and so are deconstructed. The possibilities afforded by that huge mass are then largely closed, though a new and different possibility opens. "Use it or lose it" is nature's dictum. Unfortunately, we lose about eighty percent of our potential available during that middle childhood period. One wonders what even an additional ten percent retention—which means additional middle-child development—might make to human potential.

P: How does this relate to Paul MacLean's theories about what he calls the "triune brain?"

JCP: Paul MacLean was the medical doctor in charge of the NIMH's Department of Brain Evolution and Behavior. Through decades of research he found and clearly articulated the functions of three separate brains in our heads. This is no longer considered theory but an obvious fact. On the lowest, most physical level there is the reptilian brain, which we share with all animals, reptiles, and amphibians, and which incorporates bodily movement, motor skills, sensory impressions, survival of self and species—issues of food, sex, and territorial impulses. Then there is what MacLean calls the old mammalian brain, which mankind shares with all mammals, and which governs relationship, emotions, the immune system, self-healing, learning and memory, biorhythms, and bonding. The third brain, the neo-cortex, involves creativity and intellect, and is quite huge in humans.

In a fully functioning human, there is a perfect integration and balance between the three brain systems: the R-system, or reptilian brain, involves itself only with physical activities; the limbic structure, or old mammalian brain, is concerned only with feelings and emotions; and the neo-cortex relates to what we usually call "thinking." But when these connections are not properly established, thinking often gets short-circuited, becoming emotionalism or even territorial, survival-of-the-species, violent activity: the old mammalian brain or the reptilian brain takes over.

P: You spoke of various conditions in modern life that actually seriously impede the proper development of a child's intelligence. One was that in the United States virtually all births take place in hospitals, and we don't employ midwives anymore.

JCP: Technological childbirth, involving induced labor, premature cutting of the umbilical cord, the use of pain killers for the mother, and uterine monitoring, causes damage on many different levels for the infant in later development.

Then, when there's a separation of the mother and the infant immediately after birth, a psychic shock is produced. All of this is dangerous and destructive, but these processes sometimes get institutionalized and become self-perpetuating.

P: How does this contrast with a more natural kind of childbirth, such as that practiced by traditional cultures?

JCP: There you have a bonding, based on the heart, out of which social cohesion can grow. W. G. Whittlestone, an M. D. at the University of Adelaide in Australia a few years back, was one of the first to discover a direct connection between the mother's heartbeat and the development of the embryo. A connection or link is made between the two hearts *in utero* that must be reestablished at birth. If it is, each heart sends a signal to its brain and the brain shifts its functioning accordingly, and a bond is established in the new environment, giving an underlying unity to the new diversity. Mothers throughout human history have put the infant to the left breast at birth. Left-handed mothers, right-handed mothers, it makes no difference; they put the baby next to their heart so that there is a connection between the infant heart and the heart which it has been separated from, so that in the newborn's environment, the continuity, the connection of hearts is still there.

If that doesn't happen at birth, there can be a build-up of adrenal steroids which, after about forty-five minutes, causes the infant to lose consciousness from the overload and go into shock. It takes an average of three months for nature to compensate for the damage, and we take it for granted that it's natural that there are few signs of consciousness in the child until somewhere around the tenth or twelfth week after birth. Many of the three percent of children in this country who are born at home smile immediately after birth and show rapid development, simply because they don't go into shock, but are given an environment of love and nurturing from the mother from the start.

P: What are the other factors that impede development, other than technological childbirth?

JCP: Technological childbirth is number one. Then we have day care and the collapse of the family. Day care is profoundly more damaging than most people are aware. For one thing, there is no constant role model on which the child can base his or her world views.

The model has to be constant or infant-child consciousness fragments. And finding such a constant model in day care is a problem. In a two-year study of day care in the United States, blood samples of these children across the country showed dangerously high levels of the adrenal steroids connected with stress and anxiety. When the young brain gets an overload of adrenal steroids, it goes into shock. This happens often when children under the age of four are separated from the mother for a period longer than two hours or so.

The next negative factor is television. Studies compiled by Dr. Keith Buzzell, Jerry Mander, Mary Jane Healy, and others show that the damage of television has little to do with content but rather with the pairing of imagery in synch with sound. This provides a synthetic counterfeit of what the brain itself is *supposed* to produce in response to language, as in storytelling. The child's mind becomes habituated to such sound-images, and the higher cortical structures simply shut down. Paul MacLean's work shows how in habituation the ancient reptilian brain takes over sensory processing and the rest of the brain idles along, doing nothing because it's not needed.

The brain uses the same neural structures every time the TV comes on, and very few of the higher structures are developed. They simply lie dormant, and no capacity for *creating* internal imagery develops.

P: You mentioned a wonderful quote about a little girl . . .

JCP: . . . who said she loved the pictures on radio so much more than the pictures on television because the pictures on the radio were so much more beautiful.

In storytelling, the stimulus of words brings about the production of inner images, an extraordinary creative play involving the entire brain. Each new story requires a whole new set of neural connections and reorganizations of visual activity within—a major challenge for the brain. Television, by providing all that action synthetically, is handled by the same, limited number of neural structures regardless of programming, since the brain's work has already been done for it. This is habituation. So neural potential goes unrealized and development is impaired—unless storytelling and play are provided as well as television, or preferably, *instead* of television.

Then, also, of course, television has all but eliminated radio as a story-telling medium, turning it into a mere music box. The other thing television did was to eliminate play between parents and children in about seventy percent of the American homes. It also eliminated table-talk and "grand-mother tales." All of that disappeared, and the extended family has all but disappeared.

P: You spoke a little about the importance of play, of children's games, in early development. How do labyrinthlike games, such as fox-and-hen or hide-and-seek, help children?

JCP: Organized games, like hide-and-seek or cops-and-robbers, begin in the seven-to-eleven age group. They are games where you choose up sides, and where you chase and hide. They are organized in a very loose way. A kid that age never wants to lose: even cops-and-robbers is really all just a chase, the excitement of hiding and being found and trying to find. And the rules and regulations are very loose.

But at age eleven you have a different attitude towards games: the choosing of teams itself is important. A sense of justice and fair play becomes paramount. Kids may spend an hour just choosing up sides to make sure they're fair and equally distributed. They start playing and every five minutes stop and argue passionately about infringements of the rules: "You're out!" "I was not!" "I touched you!" "You did not!" The emphasis is on setting up the rules, and then fiercely enforcing them and arguing their fairness or the fairness of their execution.

You find this in street play, vacant lot football, and sand lot baseball. The challenge in this period is to put oneself through a kind of test, a trial or ordeal. Kids are driven by a desire to get out there and slug it out. Then, too, they must come to terms with giving up individual freedom and practice self-restraint on behalf of the needs of a larger social body—the team. And this occurs as kids lose that eighty percent of the neural mass of the brain, trimming it down to "a few good men," as the Marines might say.

Today, however, there is often no longer room for kids to get together and play. Many of our planned communities do not even have sidewalks. Kids can't play out in the streets anymore; there are no sand lots. So we have "play areas" and "supervised play," in the planned communities and in the cities: after-school organizations with adults coming in with the rules and regulations and institutionalizing play.

Then after World War II came Little League. Instead of kids being out there on the sand lot passionately facing the issue of giving up their individual freedom on behalf of their larger group, we have a group of adults making every decision, drawing up all of the rules and regulations, while parents line the sides screaming, "Get him, kill him. Win at any cost." These poor grim little children, eight-, nine-, ten-year-olds, all decked out in their perfect uniforms with advertisements on their backs, following adult orders. Where now is the working-out of our social instincts and the ability to get along as a group?

P: How can parents or educators make a more positive contribution to this phase of a child's development? If the child has not had the proper kind of nurturing, can education repair this damage?

JCP: It all depends on what you're educating for. If you're only educating for a one-sided high-level intellect, or to make the child fit into an economic scheme, it's not going to do any good. The first duty of the school is to provide the child with a safe, non-threatening environment. Given that, you can't stop the brain from learning. The Waldorf schools, to a great extent, follow that pattern, as do certain other places like the Blue Rock school in Nyack, New York, and the Sudbury Valley School in Sudbury, Massachusetts, and the magnificent Workshop Way system created by Sister Grace Pilon at Xavier University in New Orleans. These systems provide the right ambience, the right environment for the child, and the proper stimulus for the proper stages of development, and then let children follow their own biorhythms of learning.

These schools establish and maintain contact with that intelligence of the heart, which is identical in every human. Then it's impossible to feel alienated, outside, or cut off from any social situation, since there's only one heart.

P: How do you mean that exactly: only one heart?

JCP: There are billions of us, each a different ego intellect up here in our head—the brain is diversity. But the intelligence of the heart is a unity. And with the proper dialogue, the proper interaction or dynamic between mind and heart, you have the proper balance between unity and diversity. We are impelled outward by diversity and our curious intellect, and yet there's always that thread back to the unified state of things, the intelligence of the heart. What is it in us that will not let us rest, that keeps us moving out? And what brings us back to what T. S. Eliot called "the still point" within? There's always the thread to let us find our way back, between unity and diversity.

P: If the brain is so complex and impelled toward diversity, how does it ever become organized at all?

JCP: There's a fascinating function in the brain they call the "target cell function." When the brain first starts forming in utero, it doesn't form as a structure but forms as a homogenized mass, a kind of "soup" of random cells. When this "soup" reaches a certain critical mass, key target cells mysteriously appear. Those target cells send out a signal for the other cells to link up with them. There are, let's say, thirty or forty billion cells in this soup, and here are these few key target cells which send out a signal which galvanizes this mass of cells. They start pushing and shoving and jostling with each other, throwing out dendrites and axons, trying to link up with the target cell. And from that simple directive, within a remarkably short period of time, this homogenized mass ends up in beautifully functional structures, each one with its own job. All the optical cells link up with the optical target cells, and the whole optical system forms in an incredibly brief time. And the auditory cells do the same thing, and so forth.

These target cells that appear are indicators of our own higher structure. Historically great figures appear who act as target cells, bringing us to new, higher structures of order. This is simply a part of the evolutionary scheme of things. They are like Ariadne with her thread. We have to move out, and we do get lost, but then this thread appears, to bring us back and up. To lead us into what? Probably another maze. Perhaps there's never a resting point; there is no such thing as nonmoving energy. Our growth may never end.

The Nature of Consciousness

An Interview with Oliver Sacks

From PARABOLA Vol. 22, No. 3, "Conscience and Consciousness"

Oliver Sacks is a professor of clinical neurology at Albert Einstein College of Medicine, and is well known for his unique insights into the functioning and inner world of patients with neurological diseases, as described in his seven books, which include **The Man Who Mistook His Wife for a Hat** (Touchstone), **Awakenings, An Anthropologist on Mars,** and **The Island of the Colorblind** (all Vintage Books).

PARABOLA: How would you define consciousness?

OLIVER SACKS: Oh, God . . . there's no warming up! That by which a person observes his or her own emotions and mental processes and conceives a sense of self—an historical and social and personal self. Along with Gerald Edelman,[1] I would distinguish a primary consciousness from a higher-order consciousness, primary consciousness being largely a perceptual awareness, and the higher-order one a conceptual notion of one's self.

P: Would you say that animals have the perceptual awareness, or not even that?

OS: I think animals can create scenes, construct scenes, perceive and endow these scenes with meaning and coherence. They're not just reacting to simple stimuli. I regard scene-making as the cardinal characteristic of a primary consciousness.

P: And then the other consciousness would be distinguished how?

OS: Partly by consciousness of death, which no animal has. Partly by the ability to recollect or to see one's life as a whole, the ability to imagine other perspectives and other states of mind, to think hypothetically and theoretically, to disenthrall oneself from the here and now.

P: Some people would make the distinction between awareness of the world and awareness of being aware. Do you think that awareness of one's self as an entity is a characteristic that only we humans have, and that it's a necessary component of the consciousness of which we're capable?

OS: The term "self-consciousness" makes it a defining component. Animals don't blush. They may not be very aware of being looked at . . . but, having said that, I think animals can have that as well: the notion that one is in another creature's "sights" is very primitive.

But I'm not sure I feel entirely capable of talking about consciousness. There have been so many books on the subject recently, a flood of them. Obviously, it's the point at which neurobiology and psychology and philosophy are going to converge.

P: And maybe physics—for a while the physicists seemed to be more interested in consciousness than the neuroscientists.

OS: Conceivably. But I'm not very sympathetic to notions of quantum consciousness, etc., insofar as they jump over all biology, and somehow see it as irrelevant. In fact, consciousness has arisen in nervous systems of a particular type and complexity, with an evolutionary history and an individual history, and it seems to me that one mustn't jump over this. I'm not saying that in principle, perhaps, consciousness couldn't go with something made of silicon rather than carbon units, as they say on *Star Trek (laugh)*. But I'm suspicious of theories of consciousness which are not rooted in a deep knowledge of the nervous system's anatomy and physiology and behavior, its embryology and evolution.

P: How do you feel about Roger Penrose's views, particularly about his main thesis that consciousness is fundamentally non-algorithmic, and that therefore a machine can never be conscious?

OS: He's clearly a genius in his own fields. But to go from the non-algorithmic quality of thinking (and I agree that "higher" mental processes are not algorithmic) to a quantum mechanical theory of consciousness seems to me a gratuitous and unnecessary jump, and an unproductive one. I think that theories of consciousness can emerge naturally and without discontinuity from existing physical and physiological laws. As to whether a machine can be conscious, it depends on how one defines "machine." There have always been mechanical metaphors of perception or consciousness, whether it was Leibniz's "mill" in the seventeenth century, the telephone exchange earlier this century, or the computer now. But I think if one is going to call the brain a machine, one must envisage a "machine" of a sort far beyond anything we ourselves can manufacture, a machine which is different in principle. I think that evolution and emergence, and learning and adaptation are built into brains, and I'm not sure there's any mechanical equivalent to these.

In 1948, when I was a teenager, I saw Grey Walter's tortoise, which was a robot programmed to respond in particular ways to particular stimuli. I can't imagine that anything like that would have any potential for consciousness. On the other hand, I think that some of Edelman's artifacts do show perceptual learning and categorization, and might, in principle, become conscious.

I'm interested by the myths of the golem, which in a way are inquiries into the question as to whether a machine can have consciousness or conscience, and if so of what sort. The first golem was made by a rabbi in Prague in the twelfth century, and designed to be a *famulus,* or domestic servant. Interestingly, the golems were mute; they didn't have language. Then some of them ran amok and killed their masters. Gershom Scholem wrote an interesting essay, called "The Two Golems," comparing the medieval golem with a computer (he was speaking at the opening of a huge new computer in Rehovot).

I've never had a feeling of even a very powerful supercomputer being conscious—whereas I have the strongest feeling of a dog being conscious. Clearly there are forms of computation, or for that matter algorithms, in some lower-level brain and mental mechanisms. Depth perception, for instance, may be explicable in terms of a relatively simple sort of repeating algorithm. And the "construction" of color, in the prestriate cortex, though more complex, is computed. But the way in which one creates scenes and meanings and gives values to things is essentially experiential and individual, and unlike anything which is done by machines. What it comes down to, I suppose, is that I will allow the computational and mechanical at many levels, but not at the highest levels.

P: This is basically all revolving around the question: what makes us conscious as opposed to all other things that seem not to be conscious, certainly not in the same way, but can do a lot of the things we do. What is the critical distinguishing feature?

OS: An organism, and especially a human organism, has to make a world, over and above reacting to specific stimuli. A dog lives in a dog's world, a bat in a bat's world. Experiences both lead to a world and are defined by it. Henry James once said that adventures happen only to those who can relate them. So, to the adventure-making mind, adventures happen; the world, indeed, largely consists of adventures. We create an inner space in which we can move relatively easily in imagination and feeling. There's a freedom of action to a considerable extent—although when one is depressed, one loses that freedom of will and also the sense that anyone else has it. There's a nice discussion in Descartes's *Meditations,* when he looks out of the window and sees people below him, and says, "They appear to have wills and choices, but how do I know they're not elaborate puppets or pieces of clockwork?" "Will" is essential in defining an organism and consciousness.

P: You mentioned earlier that the ability to imagine someone else's position, someone else's world, is part and parcel of the consciousness that we're capable of, and now you're saying that when we're depressed we lose both our own sense of freedom and also the ability to see it in anyone else. That's an interesting thing.

OS: I remember a colleague once telling me that when she was depressed, she thought other people moved in a robotic way, that it was very difficult to imagine what activated them. Similarly, when I'm depressed, poetry fails to move me. I can't enter it and it can't enter me. I see a sort of tessellated surface of words and can appreciate some of the prosodic ingenuity that has gone into it, but it leaves me cold. This can also occur in people with autism. My friend Temple Grandin, an autistic woman, is very musical, although actually she has no feeling for music. But she has high musical intelligence. She went to a concert of Bach's two- and three-part inventions, and her chief comment was she wished there had been four- and five-part inventions too! But they didn't move her in the least, although she thought them very, very ingenious.

Will. Freedom of action. Movement. I think there's an emotionality and an individuality to one's motor style. Parkinsonian festination looks mechanical and robotic, styleless and unmusical. It is seen as an "it"—"it" happens. Whereas walking is seen as an "I." I had a patient, described in *Awakenings,* a former music teacher, who said that she had been "unmusicked" by Parkinsonism, but she could be "remusicked." And I think we're partly talking about an "I" and an "it."

P: "Remusicked" how?

OS: In response to music itself. With music, she could dance, or walk with grace and arm-swing, and with a feeling of self and autonomy. She was walking naturally instead of being an object, agitated by festination. Maybe one needs to use a term like identity. Parkinsonian festination has no identity. It's anonymous. It has no style.

P: But the person still does?

OS: Yes—but gestures are very much an expression of one's identity, which is one of the reasons I found it strange and disconcerting during the filming of *Awakenings,* when Robin Williams appropriated many of my own gestures *(laugh).*

CW: This question of entering into another one's shoes, in relation to consciousness, makes it very much related to conscience. In some languages, in French, for instance, they are the same word.

OS: Yes. . . . An interesting example is Phineas Gage, a famous patient who suffered an appalling brain injury in the 1840s. Before his frontal lobes were bisected by a crowbar in an accident, he was described as a thoughtful, considerate, prudent, and farsighted man. Following his brain damage, he became reckless, improvident, thoughtless, unscrupulous, and foolish—although formal intelligence, formal cognitive powers, language and so forth, were quite preserved. It was as if he could no longer see some of the consequences of his actions, or imagine how others might see them. So there was a collapse here in both aspects of consciousness: the intellectual, and what one might call moral consciousness, or conscience.

P: Is it an inability to conceptualize, or something more subtle? I mean, if he had been asked what would happen if this or that was done, he could probably have said, but. . . .

OS: Yes, exactly. This is often brought up by Antonio Damasio,[2] that articulate frontal lobe patients can say perfectly well, perhaps, what they ought to feel. There was a judge in the First World War who had a massive frontal lobe injury which rendered him emotionless without affecting his intellectual powers. It might have been thought that this would make him a better judge, but in fact he resigned from the bench, saying that since he could no longer sympathize with or imagine the motives of anyone concerned, he felt this disqualified him. An unusual insight.

P: It reminds me of the insight your autistic friend, Temple Grandin, seems to have in terms of her own functioning.

OS: She certainly has an intellectual awareness that she lacks certain other forms of awareness. At school, she felt that there was this complex sort of intercourse, verbal and otherwise, with occult signs, intimations, and implications going on between people, to which she was not privy, and which eluded her. There was an intellectual insight, but this did not help—though it drove her to "research" human motives and minds, to become, in her words, "an anthropologist on Mars."

Is conscience only an internalization of parental discipline and social sanctions, or does there arise something transcending these, a sense of good and evil? I think there is a transcendent form of conscience, which doesn't have to do with rewards and punishments.

P: And is that something that one learns or something innate?

OS: Wittgenstein used the term "decency," i.e., whether one was a decent human being. I don't see how one could quite tell whether something like this is learned or innate, because people, apart from wolf-boys and so forth, are in the world of culture and influence from the start. It's difficult to talk about "human nature" as such, because we are invaded by culture all the while. This is one of the reasons wolf-boys are so fascinating: because of this notion that one might see human nature in the raw.

P: The visual system is clearly both innate and acquired: one is born with an innate wiring, which is massively modifiable by experience, and won't develop properly unless it's exposed to experience.

OS: Right. I would think in the same way there may be a crude sort of moral wiring, within the frontal lobes, and between these and the limbic system, etc.—the development of which may depend on complex social and moral experiences. Is "empathy," so-called, innate or acquired?

When driving I'm fascinated by thoughtless, impulsive, selfish, violent, or criminal behavior among other drivers. This arouses in me the desire to see the moral specimen more closely, so I will often catch up with such people because I want to see that moral physiognomy, their posture, the expression on their faces.

I am haunted by the notion of lies, or untruths—mine or anyone else's—including unconscious things which are almost automatic. I find, in my own work, that a lot of rewriting may sometimes be necessary to achieve a sort of moral propriety as well as an intellectual balance. With regard to lies, I met a family in California from rural Mexico, itinerant artichoke pickers, where five of the children were congenitally deaf, and had no language. They never met other people, or went to school. They had no real sign language, just a sort of "home sign" with very little grammar. They communicated among themselves and with their family and perhaps a few neighbors, but it was not a real language. And the two younger ones, a teenage boy and girl, are now learning American Sign Language. The reason I bring this up is, the girl, who is fifteen, has now become haunted by the notion of lies. She feels that she may be lying or other people may be lying—as if the acquisition of language had brought with it the concept of lying.

P: That's interesting. One can readily see that to understand lying you have to understand language. But. . . .

OS: Hughlings Jackson speaks about the fact that aphasic people, people who have lost language from brain injury, cannot make propositions, cannot think to themselves. They have just an emotional, ejaculate language.

P: Just like your artist patient who lost his color vision couldn't even imagine colors, even though intellectually he knew all about them.

On another tack, do you think there are degrees of consciousness, other than sleeping or waking?

OS: Oh yes. There are times when one is more sensitive, when one's vision is deeper, when one's vision is larger. One of the powers of art is to enlarge and deepen one's consciousness in different ways, whether it's aesthetic, or moral, or mystical consciousness. This is also a function of science and philosophy, to foster deeper and enlarged forms of intellectual consciousness. One has certain moods, or states, in which one's consciousness seems to expand and to take on a comprehending and enveloping and generous and tender, and also minute, quality, and other times when one's consciousness seems to shrink. Education should be seen as education in consciousness, and not just teaching skills.

There are many different forms of consciousness. For example, reading Simone Weil, I perceive a mystical and religious consciousness of an extraordinary order. Although it's not too available to me nor much to my taste, yet I can glimpse the place where she is at.

P: When one experiences this broadening and minuteness, isn't that in the same direction that people like her are speaking about?

OS: Perhaps so. One has exaltations. What did Flaubert say? "The mind has its erections, too." William James thought that drugs, even alcohol, were taken as mystagogues, and certainly the phrase "consciousness expansion" was very much in use in the sixties. Loss and grief can also expand one's consciousness. I wrote much of *Awakenings* immediately after my mother's death. All sorts of experiences can expand one's consciousness, and perhaps there is a mystical element.

At the end of my latest book, *The Island of the Colorblind,* I describe walking in the forest, and how the feeling of the antediluvian, of immense vistas of time, seemed to liberate me from a small, urgent, mundane selfhood into something more spacious, transcendent—a feeling of companionship with the earth, of being almost coeval with the world. It's very interesting to move among plants, animals, rocks, islands, which far antedate the human.

There was a total eclipse of the moon about three months ago. And I, who am normally too shy to speak to people in the street, ran out with my binoculars and a small telescope, saying "Look! Look!" I even intervened in a quarrel in my local parking lot—a woman was arguing with a parking attendant about something, and I said, "Stop it, you two! Stop for a minute, and look at the heavens! It's the most wonderful sight, and you won't see it again in your lifetime. Have a look, and then—if you must—you can start quarreling again." They were both so taken aback that they looked—I gave one of them the binoculars and the other one the telescope—and a brief feeling of wonder and excitement, and some sort of transcendent feeling, I think, came over them. Then they gave me back the things and went back to quarreling. *(laugh)*

Music, particularly vocal religious music, such as Bach, sometimes transports me to spheres and states of consciousness which would not be accessible otherwise. I was overwhelmed when I went to Jonathan Miller's St. Matthew Passion last Sunday. Jonathan Miller is a very old friend of mine, and like myself is a Jewish atheist. And yet this Jewish atheist had got together a most ravishing, deeply moving vision of the Passion.

It is similar with the visual arts. After looking at Vermeers and saturating myself, I may get into a Vermeer mood, and see light and shadows and human postures as never before.

When I was in South Africa, I met a near-namesake—it turned out that our grandfathers were from the same part of Lithuania—a man called Albie Sachs. He's a very close friend of Nelson Mandela's, and like Mandela, he has been through a great deal—he had his whole arm blown off in an assassination attempt. But he is completely without bitterness or resentment, as Mandela is. I was awed by being with him. I felt I was in the presence of a moral genius, an extraordinary being, with a transcendent expanded moral consciousness . . . conscience. And just by going for a walk with him, I think I absorbed a little bit of it, as one may go for a walk with a very sensitive or poetic person and begin to share their vision for a while; and perhaps some residue is left.

P: Even going for a walk with someone who is a stranger to where one is walking, one can experience the scenery as if it were new.

OS: Absolutely. Every human contact can potentially change one's consciousness, because one is encountering a view of the world and a construction of the world different from one's own.

P: Are you really an atheist?

OS: Oh, I don't know.

P: I'm reminded of your phrase "apprehending the first composer," which is such a nice phrase.

OS: Actually I think I was quoting Sir Thomas Browne—that was in "The Twins" [in *The Man Who Mistook His Wife for a Hat*]. And quite a lot of religious, mystical stuff got into the leg book [*A Leg to Stand On*]. But I can't quite imagine myself back into some of those states of mind. I feel no need, and I see no room for, a caretaker, a heavenly Father, or anything other than what science deals with. I have no sense of a Design or Purpose. On the other hand, I feel, to paraphrase Darwin, that there is a sort of grandeur in the vision of evolution. But it's not the sort of grandeur which can be as emotionally satisfying or which can call to a person in the same way as, say, Giotto's paintings in the Scrovegni Chapel, with their depiction of a man-centered cosmos and a heaven in which someone looks down on you, and pays attention to you. I can't imagine any sort of personal deity.

P: The idea of a God that looks down on you specifically is one non-atheist view, but one can also regard oneself as smaller than a cell in terms of any attention that would be individually allotted and still have a sense of some sort of purpose.

OS: Yes, in some sense one contributes to the history of the universe. . . . But having said all this, I find that words like heaven and hell, and blessing and curse, and prayer, and thanksgiving, are often in my mouth. I keep a Bible as well as a dictionary on my bedside table. I can't say I read it just as literature, or because I enjoy the language of the King James version, although I do; perhaps it's a bit like Vermeer or Bach, granting one at least vicarious entry into another world or many other worlds. I think one needs an attitude of gratitude at being alive, and a feeling of being blessed or privileged to be here at all, to have one's senses, to be in fairly good health. I'm not quite sure what to call that feeling. It's not just a moral feeling. I often want to give thanks—to whom? for what? I like working in religious atmospheres, and I work every Wednesday morning in a Jewish hospital and Wednesday afternoons in a Catholic home.

P: In Indian medical thinking, the mind is regarded as another sense organ. You're describing a relationship with the world that requires the mind, because the mind can know the significance of what I see; and at the same time it requires something more, because the mind by itself doesn't lead to that sort of feeling.

OS: When I feel good, I feel like a growing shoot, and it's this feeling of being a growing shoot, this biological image, which for me is the image of consciousness and conscience, and not any sort of mechanical image. Winnicott used to feel that there was within everyone something like this—he would compare it to a tulip—some autonomous, unique identity, inaccessible to consciousness, protected against intervention or interference in most normal ways, and he felt it was part of the business of analysis to keep clear of this. I think one of the reasons I like plants is the feeling of their persisting in their own being, and not being, as it were, sponges for social influences or whatever.

I get most of my metaphors from the biological world, and a surprising number from the vegetable world. People will immediately say, "well, we're animals," and go for animal metaphors, but I think the vegetable notion of the growing shoot is a good symbol for consciousness. I respond more to the natural world than to the modern cultural and human worlds. Whether it's the stars or the forest or scuba diving in coral reefs, I feel these as expanding consciousness.

NOTES

1. Dr. Edelman, director of the Neurosciences Institute and chairman of the Department of Neurobiology at the Scripps Research Institute, has written a number of books on the neural basis of consciousness. His views emphasize the biological and evolutionary nature of the human brain and mind. He has also created several computer-based artifacts which simulate some aspects of human mental activity.

2. Dr. Damasio, professor and chairman of the Department of Neurology at the University of Iowa College of Medicine, is recognized worldwide as a leader in the study of the effects of brain damage on mental activity. His 1994 book, *Descartes' Error,* emphasizes the role of emotion in human cognition and rationality, and contains a detailed description of the case of Phineas Gage, who was a seminal case for understanding the role of the frontal lobes in man.

Confronting Our Humanity

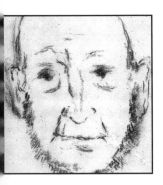

The Human Face

Point of Return

We Are All
Witnesses

FREDERICK FRANCK

URSULA K. LE GUIN

ELIE WIESEL

Vol. 23, No. 3
"Fear"

Vol. 23, No. 1
"Millennium"

Vol. 10, No. 2
"Exile"

The Human Face

An Interview with Frederick Franck

From PARABOLA Vol. 23, No. 3, "Fear"

> **Frederick Franck,** a consulting editor to **PARABOLA**, is the author of numerous books, including **Zen Seeing, Zen Drawing** (Bantam) and **Pacem in Terris: A Love Story** (Codhill Press). He lives in Warwick, New York, where he has converted an eighteenth-century mill ruin into a transreligious sanctuary.

PARABOLA: What is fear? Where does fear come from?

FREDERICK FRANCK: If I am to speak of fear, which is less an academic than an existential matter, I'd better be fearlessly personal.

I was five years old when on August 4, 1914, half a mile south of our doorstep and just across the Dutch-Belgian border, the Kaiser's armies invaded Belgium. I saw the next town, Vise, go up in flames, and the endless stream of refugees and wounded and dying soldiers started to pass our windows. The twentieth century had started in earnest, and if I am still around on New Year's Eve in the year 2000, I'll have lived almost the full length of it, facing fear in all its varieties—but not only fear, not only the horrors, but also the overwhelming beauty and joy of being alive.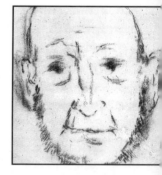

What is this fear? Obviously a state of disquiet, of powerless apprehension, intensified into dread of ever-impending disasters, of mortal dangers, of imminent annihilation: a dread that may explode into panic, causing the acute distress in which our neuromuscular system is either immobilized or else goes into mindless spasms of flight between unyielding, unscalable walls of terror.

P: What is your greatest experience of fear?

FF: From my fifth to my ninth year, in constant fear, I looked as from a neutral grandstand, our Dutch side of the border, into hell. When World War I ended in 1918, there was famine in Germany, just a few miles to the east. Soon the first rumblings of Nazism became audible, and the Belgians started to dig the strategic Albert Canal right on that border, slicing through a three-hundred-foot-high sandstone hill. Its vertical walls were studded with gun emplacements and machine gun nests, facing east towards Germany. That was in 1929, and it predicted the Second World War which was to follow ten years later, when the Nazi tanks circumvented this static northern anchor of the Maginot Line on their drive for Paris.

I seemed to be totally isolated in my fear, a fear that was specific, focused on nightmarish realities that soon proved themselves to be more than horrifying. It was a fear that was almost the opposite of anxiety, that unease about undefined, perhaps imaginary calamities. The people around me seemed blind to it all; they called me a pessimist, and mocked me as being obsessed.

P: Sometimes fear paralyzes, sometimes it galvanizes. What makes the difference?

FF: Fear, perception, and imagination must be closely connected. I must have been blessed or cursed with too much of all of them, for I saw the phantasmagoria that was to follow as clearly and graphically as Hieronymus Bosch saw the monsters of his age in his chilling visions. It was this imagination that made me take a boat and cross the Atlantic, still wondering whether my fears were not primal atavisms, the kind of terror that makes horses bolt at sudden shadows, makes herds stampede for some riddlesome reason, makes cockroaches scatter at the approach of the foot that will crush them. On the safe side of the Atlantic I tasted lesser fears: fear of the automatisms of a foreign culture, fear of social disapproval, of having the wrong accent, of trespassing against the etiquette—or the lack of it—in these new surroundings.

Many of these personal perturbations of the threatened ego disappeared through the years, but an overarching fear, no less justified than that which dominated me during the years before World War II, remains—more precisely, increases—as we approach the Third Millennium after Golgotha: the climate changes, the ever-increasing violence, the diabolical inventions of technology, with no *deus ex machina* in sight. . . .

P: Is there a difference between fear of Caesar and fear of the Lord?

FF: I must confess that in my case there is not so much a fear of the Lord, of Ultimate Reality, as a deep reverence, a profound awe of the Mystery of mysteries that is sheer Existence, and an uninterrupted astonishment at being here at all as Wondrous Being—able to discern, however vaguely, the Laws that rule the universe confirmed, and with them the moral structure of reality, the *Dharmakaya*. And as far as Caesar is concerned: one's fears are more than justified, for Caesar's power is arbitrary, whether this Caesar is a person, a state, or a combination of multinationals. It is rooted in delusions, in denial of the limits of power and of the human mortality of whosoever wields it. It is the kind of mindless power that characterizes the inflated ego, to which it is prudent to pay the required respects, for it is prudent not to challenge the arrogance of power, be it that of Time-Warner, of Caesar, or that of his deputy, the traffic cop.

Moreover, ruthless and frightful as the inflated ego may be, it is the collectivized ego, the in-group ego, whether national, ethnic, or religious, that is always poised for barbarism and massacre. The only defense here is timely flight.

P: Can fear play any role in respect to inner growth?

FF: Allow me to replace "growth" by "maturation" or "individuation" or even "emancipation." The concept of "growth" is all too overstretched in both psychology and economics. For me, "growth" is associated with the tendency to degenerate into malignancy. Small is beautiful! Maturation opens quite different perspectives, uses no measuring sticks or at most takes soundings of depth.

P: Why is there so much fear in the world today? Has this always been so?

FF: I would point at the cockroach phenomenon: the awareness that our very existence is in jeopardy, that we may be on the road to terminal disaster, and that our science and technology have proven to be perversions. We have addled the meaning of life, ignored the life span of living things (our own included), "conquered" space by our insane compulsion for acceleration, disturbed the cosmic rhythms, and made nature the victim of a limitless greed that is incompatible with our survival—in particular our survival as a human species. It is high time to become aware of the problems of technology not as technological problems, but as human problems, and to realize that tinkering with a perverted, almost cannibalistic system will not prevent the condemnation of three-quarters of the human population to subhuman existence in the next few decades. Perhaps our all-too-justifiable fear could still stimulate an intensified questioning of what it means to be human and thereby recoup the Human Imperative.

P: Is there a relationship between love or compassion and fear?

FF: I can't help thinking here of "Before Abraham was, I AM," which somehow dates the Human Imperative back to the cosmic event of anthropoid mutating into Adam, the Anthropos, a process still far from completed, so that our science and technology are nothing but sophisticated anthropoids concocting pollution, germ warfare, and nuclear holocausts. The Human Imperative is that which makes me recognize the human face in the other, in each one of the others. Two visions spring to mind here: that of the eighth-century Buddhist sage Hui Neng, who confronted his disciples with the challenge, "Show me the face you had before even your parents were born," and that of the fifteenth-century Christian mystic Nicholas of Cusa, who saw "in all faces the Face of faces, veiled as in a riddle." Both saw the archetypically Human. So in our time does Emmanuel Levinas, who teaches at the Sorbonne, and who sees in the human face, in the defenseless naked eyes of the other, the epiphany of our archetypal humanness.

I remember clearly how during the horrors of World War I (I was still in grade school), I started a constant questioning about attitudes and acts that would stamp one as human and others as less than human. I judged my teachers according to what I perceived as their humanness. It came naturally. The question "What does it mean to be human?" has preoccupied me throughout life as the one central question in relation to which all other questions—political, economic, artistic, spiritual—proved to be secondary. My writing, but even more, my lifelong preoccupation with *seeing* as contrasted to "looking-at" the world—my seeing/drawing, my sculptures, the building of my sanctuary Pacem in Terris—are all attempts at answering that central question.

The great religious traditions point at the answer: not a single one of them commands "Thou shalt kill, cheat, torture, exploit." Yet in their practice they—the Abrahamic ones in particular—have contradicted the empathy, compassion, and humanness they have preached through the centuries. They have fallen for the arrogance of the inevitable in-group barbarity.

I can't help thinking here about the function of the prefrontal cortex in defining the specifically human, in particular the neurobiology of the triune brain as described by Paul D. MacLean. It is one of the rare instances in which science confirms the criteria of our specific humanness. The prefrontal cortex, the latest outcropping of the human brain, includes our awareness of our own life process. No other animal seems to have this awareness, which makes identification with other life processes possible and may cause the first inklings of empathy, from which may flower compassion and foresight. Fear may be a stimulant of the awareness of human solidarity—even identification with all that lives—and hence of unsentimental compassion.

To me, somehow, the nonphilosopher Levinas confirms MacLean's findings on the prefrontal cortex's potential for empathy and compassion: a *sui generis* ethics that precedes all thinking, in which ego takes the place of the other and becomes the Self, hostage of the other's suffering, the other's reality. At the apex of barbarism, is the meaning of being human confirmed? At the saturation point of evil, does the Dove of the spirit take wing?

Point of Return

An Interview with Ursula K. Le Guin

From PARABOLA Vol. 23, No. 1, "Millennium"

Ursula K. Le Guin is the award-winning author of many books, including the **Earthsea** novels (Bantam Spectra), **The Left Hand of Darkness** (Ace Books), and an original interpretation of the **Tao Te Ching** (Shambhala).

PARABOLA: Why are we attracted to the story of the millennium?

URSULA K. LE GUIN: In my mind, the millennium is not a story, but a point. It's like the *bindu* in Hindu terminology, the invisible point. If the millennium is any part of a story, it's not the story itself, but the end, the wrap-up. It certainly has religious connotations: isn't the millennium the epiphany, the arrival of God and the end of time? Or am I exaggerating?

P: The bindu is the end, as you say, but it is also that from which everything originates.

UKL: Like the universal core for the Big Bang, if you go for the Big Bang theory. Yes, it's sort of everything *in potentia,* but nothing yet. . . .

P: And the millennial point is like that?

UKL: In the sense of being a vanishing point. What is it? It's nothing. It's just another year, you know. The real year lies in its cyclicalness, in the seasons and in the movements of the earth among the stars, the solstices and the equinoxes. That, to me, is the reality of the year. Then we attach numbers to these years, and one of them turns out to be the year one thousand. There's an arbitrariness to that number which I can't get away from.

P: In the cycle, is there a human need for a new beginning?

UKL: Absolutely. Everybody celebrates some kind of new year, right? Everybody has celebrations of the cycle of the year, such as harvest festivals and the great solstice festivals.

In one of my science fiction novels, *The Left Hand of Darkness,* there's a people for whom every year is the year one. They count past time as the year One-Ago, Two-Ago. . . . They don't have a fixed dating system. Something that was five hundred years ago last year is five hundred and one years ago this year. Their history, obviously, is fluid. I was trying to catch the idea that *every* year is the year one: it starts fresh, and the numbers attached to it are arbitrary. I was trying to play with the idea of time.

P: How do these people conceive of the future?

UKL: The reference point keeps changing. But they certainly plan ahead. They could make a five-year plan in their economy; they would just refer to it a little bit differently.

P: Would these people have a need to think apocalyptically?

UKL: Evidently they don't. As they appeared to me, these are people living in a world during an ice age, under very severe circumstances where life is a fairly fragile, difficult matter. You never get really warm. . . . They built up a civilization, cities and all that, but they have a fairly pragmatic approach to life, forced upon them in a sense by the climate. Their sexuality is another matter, but I think that has nothing to do with their time sense. Maybe it does, on the other hand, because they're all androgynous.

These people live forcefully in the present. Although they have history and although they look forward, they don't seem to have the apocalyptic mindset. They've also never had a war; that could have something to do with it. The bad things that come to them come from the nature of their world, rather than from their own doings. They have lots of fights and quarrels and murders, and so on—I mean, they're human—but they have not organized themselves to make war. One of the apocalyptic events therefore doesn't occur.

P: Is there a need to purge the memory, and because of that the apocalyptic idea comes to the surface? I'm fascinated with the idea of a people who can do without history.

UKL: Haven't most of us largely done without history? As I understand, most people before modern industrial culture did not have a history for longer than a couple of generations. They had stories about the year the stars fell, or they kept a year count, like the Lakota, which might go back fifty or sixty years, but not much longer. And before that was dreamtime, was mythtime. Is that time really "before"? Or is it "the other time"?

P: Yes, as Eliade speaks of, *in illo tempore*. Or faerie time.

UKL: Very frequently in Native American world pictures, there is a dreamtime, the other time, in which, for one thing, people and animals are absolutely not distinguished. All beings are of the same order. And then comes the change, when, as in the Yurok stories for instance, it's quite clear that time alters. Coyote says things like "when we come to the time of change, when the people take over." Now there's a millennium for you! Not in the sense of a thousand years, but in the sense of an absolute change into a different kind of time. There's the time when they're getting the world ready, and then there's the time when the inheritors, the human people, take over.

P: I was thinking of parallels to those native stories in something like Norse myth, with Ragnarok, or even in the direction that Tolkien takes it with the wars before the age of Middle-Earth, in *The Silmarillion*.

UKL: Tolkien has a series of endings and new beginnings. I must say, though, that I never really believed very much in the rebirth after Ragnarok. I took those stories very, very seriously as a child; they were the mythologies that spoke to me most, the Norse myths in Padraic Colum's retelling. And I saw Ragnarok in the future, in my future, as something that was yet to come. It was a story that had not yet been told, and when it happened that would be the end, by golly! I saw it as a complete tragedy. The myth tells about two survivors, and the world being reborn, but I didn't believe it. So there was an apocalypse that I was willing to accept as a valid, tragic story about life.

P: I suppose Tolkien's version is much more optimistic.

UKL: Despite the fact that it's an enormous fantasy, Tolkien puts his soul firmly into the reality of ordinary life, because the hobbits are at the center. Which is, I think, what makes *The Lord of the Rings* enormously more meaningful than *The Silmarillion*. *The Silmarillion* is very beautiful and strange and wonderful—lord, I wish I'd read it when I was thirteen!—but *The Lord of the Rings* is a real novel, a book about life. The fact that the hobbits are ordinary people doing ordinary things grounds the enormous tragic event in a way that makes me able to believe that life goes on after it.

Perhaps we could say that *The Silmarillion* is in illo tempore, and we get into real time with *The Lord of the Rings*. Blake's prophetic books, which are marvelous poetry, take place in outside time, like *The Silmarillion*. I never thought of it before, but the books share something of the same enormous vision, that larger-than-life visionary quality.

P: So the notion behind the millennium is an absolute change into a different kind of time. Since some of us have a kind of rare, exceptional experience of a different kind of time in our otherwise ordinary lives, is there a correspondence to the millennium? Could we talk about a personal millennium?

UKL: I was thinking about this subject during the last couple of weeks—what a "personal millennium" would mean to me. It would mean the age of seventy *(laughter)* from which I am now two years away. You see, I keep perceiving a millennium as closure, in a sense, as end. And "in my end is my beginning," always, but still. . . .

P: Your belief in Ragnarok.

UKL: Also the traditional Western mindset, which is always looking for endings. We're apocalypse-obsessed people.

P: We have a difficult time thinking acausally.

UKL: Very difficult. We prefer not to think cyclically; we prefer to think that we did something and it's done once and for all. Then you start fresh on something entirely different. But there's a kind of drasticness to that. I've had trouble with the word "apocalypse" for years, because science fiction, which I write, has been defined as apocalyptic fiction. And my books aren't apocalyptic. I reject that mindset. *(laughter)* Life goes on, you know.

P: Is there a conception of a millennium that isn't so fraught with apocalypse?

UKL: Oh, I think so, going back to the religious sense of the word, the sense of the new revelation, or the arrival of God on earth. There are also Utopian conceptions of the millennium. Unfortunately, they're things like the Thousand-Year Reich. We will have peace and glory and Aryan domination on earth for a thousand years—well, excuse me, but I think not!

P: If there's a movement of being reabsorbed into the bindu, this point through which a different time is felt, are there changes of mind as a millennium is neared? In Hindu India, the bindu was also a point of concentration.

UKL: Right. It's a meditational device. A support.

P: If we think of the millennium in relation to that, then is there correspondingly a concentration in the minds of the human race, or at least in some of us?

UKL: That's a hard question. I mean, if you look back historically, the century before the year 1000 in Europe was a time of considerable hysteria, wasn't it?

P: Do you have a sense of the acceleration of time?

UKL: Well, you know, time gets weird as you get older—it speeds up and slows down in unexpected ways. Yet everybody that's lived in the twentieth century feels that it has accelerated. My mother and my mother-in-law were both born around 1900; they started out with buggies, with horses. My father was born in 1875—he saw enormous changes. And the pace of the change has seemed always to accelerate. And now. . . we fill time so full.

I had empty time as a teenager. Every summer was a vast, empty space that I filled as I pleased. I don't see any teenagers with that leisure anymore. There are things they have to do, places they have to be, programs. . . . Then there's the television and the computer, they have a connection there that didn't exist when I was a kid. It fills the world so solid, I sometimes wonder if they ever get a deep breath, or feel what it's like to have a whole afternoon with nothing to do. One thing that put this in mind was re-reading *Huckleberry Finn* recently. The vastness of the days that those boys had! It was up to them to fill them—and they did, God knows. It's in that sense that time has shrunk to the ticking clock time that we all live by. I never take off my wristwatch. I'm totally caught by it.

P: Has the other time receded from the surface of the planet, in all the frenetic pace and busyness?

UKL: I do think that's part of the sickness that lies on us, yes. Because we have history but not myth. Only through art do most people find it. Listening to music, you enter the other time. Music makes its own time, literally. When you read a novel, you are living in another time. It's not *the* other time; it's not in illo tempore, but it's our version of it. All arts create the time outside of time, which is not clock-time. It is, in a sense, dreamtime. We do have that, and we have more of that than anybody has ever had. We have enormous access to the arts.

P: Do you feel that there is still a consciousness of what the arts and music and even the dream serve?

UKL: I think there is a strong consciousness of that. Sometimes it gets a little woo-woo. The New Age apprehension of it can be a little too facile, but it's on the right track. What's on the wrong track is television, the mindless babble that people leave on and sort of semi-watch. It doesn't take them into any other time; it just cuts up present time into these weird little sections interspersed with advertisements. Children's Saturday morning television makes my hair stand on end. It's a segmentation and a fragmentation of time which is . . . I don't see how kids survive it. They do—kids are really tough— and they come out more or less sane. But I think it's a real victory that they do.

P: I hear a note of hopefulness, that the hunger for entry into another time has not been really satisfied and persists even in the media-ridden world of today.

UKL: The hunger persists and therefore often finds its real food, but we do make it hard sometimes for kids to realize that there *is* real food, literally or aesthetically speaking: that there is real nourishment, offered by other human beings just like them.

P: Is there anything we haven't touched on yet, that you'd like to say in conclusion?

UKL: I would like to throw in the nice Taoist word "return." Perhaps any milepost such as a millennium is not only an end and a beginning, but can also be part of a cycle, a part of return. The journey, to me, because I read Lao Tse very early, has always lain in returning.

We Are All Witnesses

An Interview with Elie Wiesel

From PARABOLA Vol. 10, No. 2, "Exile"

Elie Wiesel, Holocaust survivor, author, and teacher, lives in New York City, and since 1976 has served as Andrew W. Mellon Professor in the Humanities at Boston University. He has received numerous honorary degrees and awards, including the 1986 Nobel Peace Prize, and is the author of more than forty books.

PARABOLA: Exile and the return from exile can be seen from many different levels. When the feeling appears of not quite belonging here, of being a stranger, that can be the beginning of a movement of return. What do you see as the real exile?

ELIE WIESEL: I cannot see any other exile but the real exile, and that exile is total. It envelops all endeavors, all explorations, all illusions, all hopes, all triumphs, and this means that whatever we do is never complete. Our life is not complete, and lo and behold, our death is not complete: one does not die when one should, or the way one should. As you know, in our tradition we speak of exile in absolute categories. Exile envelops God Himself; God Himself is in exile. Language is in exile. The *Shekhinah*, of course, is supposed to be everywhere, and it is exile that carries it everywhere. So exile for us is something which is as absolute, as infinite, as life.

P: There is a feeling of being cut off, and yet there can be a thread, no more than a little thread to someone or something higher than oneself. When that is cut, that is the exile, don't you think?

EW: Not necessarily. For example, exile has a link to solitude—why? Because we are away from home, we are away from our memories, we are away from security. But what is easier to bear—to be in exile alone, or with someone whom one loves? It may become worse to see the other person also suffering. So maybe the cutoff is a blessing and not a curse. One of the reasons why so many Hasidic rebbes sank into melancholy was precisely the *Galut ha-Shekhinah*, the Exile of the Shekhinah. They were ready to bear their own suffering, but not the suffering of God.

P: Is that your understanding today, or did they express that in their own way?

EW: It's my understanding, which they didn't express. I discovered their melancholy, I was struck by it, and I couldn't understand why it was so. The greatest of the Hasidic masters, meaning the first generation, the companions and disciples of the Besht, all of them without any exception at one point in their lives had an encounter with melancholy, with deep depression. And I couldn't understand it, because all of them were speaking of joy and happiness and exhilaration. Why should they be in such danger of falling into depression? I studied it, I researched every case, always in their terms, with their books and stories. And the reason was a *transfer,* a transfer in the sense that they didn't encounter depression on their own account but because of the separation of the Shekhinah. And that's something, after all. If I suffer, maybe I've done something, but if God suffers, what right do I have to suffer for Him?

The real exile, the profound exile—where did it begin? It began with Adam, who fled God, and with Cain, who fled human beings. Or did it begin with Abraham, who fled his parents, or with Moses, who fled his enemies? There are categories in exile. God's exile also has many stages. In the Kabbalah, we read that God's exile—the Breaking of the Vessels—occurred very far back, at Creation. The Creation and exile were almost simultaneous. In the Midrash, we read that it happened during the destruction of the Temple, the first destruction.

P: God's exile from what?

EW: We don't know about that, we only knew that *we are* in exile; that, we know. And we ask ourselves, how did God our Father allow this to happen? There are many answers given. One answer was that God Himself is suffering.

P: Terrible trials and tests have been put in the way of the Jewish people, which are inseparably bound up with exile. After the concentration camps, someone said, "God saw that it was enough." After two thousand years, the Jews could return to their land. Does this mean the exile is over?

EW: The entire period is a question. I envy those who think that God said it is enough. Maybe He said it's only a warning. I'm scared, I'm literally scared for the future of mankind. It seems to be the plan that whatever happens to the Jews later happens to the world. God gave the Law to all the peoples; we were the first to accept it, and then we shared it. Almost every phase in our civilization we later shared because we wanted to share; for after all, God said "I am your God," and we said, "Thank you, but don't be our God alone, be everyone's God." He gave the Torah, we are told in our tradition: He went from one people to another, from one nation to another, and nobody wanted it. And again, we accepted it—under duress, but we accepted. The moment we accepted, He said: everybody gets it!

There is a tendency in us: the more Jewish we want to be, the more universal we become. That is true in everything. There is a thesis to be elaborated about the connection, let's say, between the Inquisition in Spain and what happened to Spain, between the exodus of the Jews from Spain and the downfall of Spain. Somehow, when Jews left the country, it fell into bad shape. Very often, in Europe, they called them back.

P: What we've been talking about so far has more to do with all of us, with human beings in general. But when it comes to a man's own work on himself, then things have to be looked at in quite another way. A man learns enough about himself to see that something is lacking. He needs to live in the present, and not worry about past history or the future. Maybe the first thing he has to understand is that something in him is in exile from his true self.

EW: Yes, but what you say about having no concern for past history or the future is impossible. How could human beings be human without the past?

P: Yes, but what about the present moment when I can *be?*

EW: What is exile? What is *galut?* Whenever I have a problem, I go to the original Hebrew idioms. After all, the world was created in that language. Let's go back to the relations of that word: *gal*, move, *gil*, joy: it means *movement*, continuous movement. It means that everything is moving, except me; or the other way—I am moving and everything else stands still; or still a third way, we are not moving in the same direction. Then exile means to be displaced, I am here and I am not here. The content and form do not espouse one another. That means they are in exile. When a person is in exile, nothing fits.

P: Do you see a purpose in the exile?

EW: We are told there is a purpose, the purpose is redemption. This is expressed in the Kabbalistic theory of the Gathering of the Sparks, after which the universe itself will be redeemed.

P: The Jewish people have had experiences which, had they stayed in one place, might never have occurred. And the rest of the world has had experiences because of the Jews which it might never have had. From the point of view of a return, could there have been something useful there?

EW: Do you ask my opinion or the opinions of other people whom I could quote? In my personal opinion, I cannot bring myself to find a purpose to suffering, so much suffering. I am ready to accept my suffering, but not the suffering of others. Does it have a purpose, was it useful, two thousand years of suffering?

P: Yet there are individual stories of men growing as a result of their suffering. People suffer intentionally, perhaps, to reach another level, to come closer to God.

EW: You find that phenomenon in every mystical movement: the self-inflicted wounds, suffering to reach a higher level, a higher sphere; then, variations occurred, you joined your suffering to the suffering of Christ, or you suffered for God, but it's still self-inflicted suffering. We never accepted it. You know in the Bible, when somebody renounces the usual, normal, everyday joys of life, he must make a sacrifice in atonement.

P: You said that the goal of exile is redemption. What does that mean?

EW: I am told, I didn't invent it. My feeling is really that we did not choose exile, we never did. As long as we were in exile, we tried to rationalize it, and to see it in a larger context. We weren't satisfied to say that because Israel was in exile, the redemption would be only the redemption of Israel, a geographic redemption. We wanted to return to the Kingdom of David. In other words, we wanted the impossible. Only the impossible could explain or accept or justify so many sufferings. We speak of exile, and we speak of Messianic redemption, which is universal redemption—not only of the Jewish people but of Creation itself. And then all the imageries are possible: the wolf and the lamb at peace, there will be no slaves, justice will prevail.

P: Is there an exile within Judaism itself—not the exile of Jews in the diaspora versus Jews in Israel, but an exile within the religion? The religion of the successful American Jew often seems very dilute, and yet there is a longing to return to a more authentic Judaism. Have authentic Jews reached out to these economically successful and religiously failed Jews?

EW: I don't know them! I know quite a few young people whom I teach (and I love them), who have a profound, authentic quest for something truthful. Not only in my classes at Boston University, but wherever I go, I meet people who want something. But there is no support anymore. The future is frightening, it is frightening.

I had to give a lecture in a seminar on the Year 2000. My topic was the future of language. So I worked on it, and never have I had to work so hard on a lecture, because at that time I couldn't imagine the Year 2000. Yet it was only fifteen years away! Is this the feeling of the millennium? I'm not sure. It's the feeling that we are racing too fast; technologically, scientifically, we're going too fast, and in ethics and in philosophy we remain behind. Technology is never really pure, it's always at the expense of something. Maybe that is what the young people are afraid of—they see themselves running, thrusting into the future at a tremendous pace, and they look for support in the past, which is there, and the past after all is synonymous with survival; we survived the past. But can we survive the future?

P: Until modern times, traditions and customs made it possible for people to have more or less tolerable lives; they supported people, the possibility of living closer to one's center was there. Now, there is such a collapse of many traditions. You and a few other authors have restored the Hasidic tradition—

EW: Well, I have not; I have tried to tell a few stories.

P: It seems as if, in the absence of traditions, the master is terribly important—the single individual who concentrates the knowledge and whose very presence in a room changes the way people think and feel.

EW: Absolutely, absolutely, look at the Besht: when he came to a town, the simple fact that he was there influenced people. Moses—I would be afraid to meet Moses, but I would like to meet him. He was the one who was a watershed in everything, not only to his disciples but to all the people that he and his disciples had never met.

P: Is there a teacher to send people to now—a spiritual guide?

EW: Ah, this is a disturbing question. I am looking for one. My own case is different, because I *had* teachers. The longing is not only for teachers but for what they represent, a whole world.

Hasidism is very beautiful, but to me it's amazing to see Hasidism in New York. It's so atypical here. Hasidism had to be in villages; it was born in villages, it was meant for villages. Hasidism is not only a structure of perceptions or of melodies or of stories, it is a geography. It had to be in the mountains of Carpathia, and in the villages there that were abandoned and forsaken. It was never a city movement, it was a village movement. You know, some streets in Brooklyn are structured like the villages in Eastern Europe. But the fact is that the Hasidic movement suffered most of the losses. I think three Masters survived among hundreds and hundreds.

P: There is a sense in which Hasidism was very healthy and alive even in 1930, but in your books you have also implied that there was a decline after the first three generations in the Hasidic movement.

EW: I confess, I glorify them. I do it with love, because whenever I have to repeat something negative it hurts me so much. If I had written my books in the 1930s, like Martin Buber, I would have become an objective, neutral, critical historian of normative Hasidism; why not? But today this wouldn't do them justice. Of course, I know the truth—the first and second generations, and the third, were great. The fourth was less great.

P: The third generation was trained by the Great Maggid?

EW: Yes, and then began the dynasties, families, and everywhere you found children becoming heads of schools. It was no longer in the tradition of the Besht. The Besht's successor was not his son, but a disciple. Moses left his succession not to his children but to his disciple Joshua. That is the tradition: it goes from master to disciple, not from master to son. But in later Hasidism, it went from father to son.

P: So that people wouldn't fight and envy each other?

EW: They fought! Why? Because really the generations became less worthy.

P: Isn't there always the "chain of tradition"? Doesn't *someone* always appear to maintain the life behind Judaism or behind any tradition—the *melamed vav* in Jewish tradition?

EW: The melamed vav is by definition unknown. But that doesn't matter. There are always masters, but they change. That is of the very essence of Judaism. How was the tradition handed down? Moses gave it to the Elders, the Elders to the Judges, the Judges to the Prophets, then to the Teachers, then to other Teachers. Every generation has had its paradigmatic personage. Somehow, Jewish history has always managed to find those who kept it alive.

P: There has been something Biblical about recent Jewish history, hasn't there?

EW: I think we live in Biblical times. This is the conclusion I have reached. We live in extraordinary times.

P: To see through the inner exile, to find oneself deeply happy to be here and to be what one is, accepting whatever burdens and suffering there may be—this requires a great deal of intensity. Where is the intensity in Judaism today? Where is the real quest?

EW: Our times are Biblical, but also paradoxical. On one hand, you may say we have never been so poor because of what we have lost; on the other, when you see what is going on in Jewish life, it's amazing. Never has Talmud been taught in so many places as it is being taught now. Never has there been such growth. Never has Hasidism been so popular. People want to study, they want to come along to communities.

In France, all those young people in 1968 who belonged to the Maoists, the Trotskyites, etc.—what are they doing now? They are studying Talmud! Jean-Paul Sartre's adopted daughter just published a translation of *Eyn Ya'akov*, a huge Midrashic work. You can't imagine what's happening there.

P: Abraham Heschel once said that the "school" in the sense of "school of the prophets" is missing in Judaism.

EW: It's difficult to evaluate, for geographic reasons again. In a small city with 15,000 Jews, sixty or seventy *shuls*, houses of prayer and study, it was easy—easier than it can be in New York or Chicago or Los Angeles. Here we need other methods. But the new methods must never be against the orthodox; a new method must be an outgrowth of orthodoxy but never against it. If the Talmud had been against the Prophets, there would be no Talmud; the Talmud came to complement. If the Midrash later came against the Talmud, it would never have grown; if Rashi had been *against*—but never *against*; it's always an adjustment, but not in opposition to. A new method is possible, it is necessary. We have to remember that we need also strong roots.

P: May I ask: you have been a witness, and—

EW: We are all witnesses, I have no privilege.

P: But you have witnessed such things as most people don't see. As a witness, you help us all to remember: what is it we should remember?

EW: Everything! We have to remember that we can't remember. My fear really is that memory is in exile. The only possible salvation of the Jewish people is to remember our whole experience. But this memory is so powerful, so exalted, that we can't remember fully: it is bigger than us, bigger than all of us, than all the people. So how do you transform it into memory? Memory must not stop. If I were to stop in, let's say, 1944, it would lead to madness. And then I realize that, after all, there was a Jewish life before, and there I find my friends and my teachers, and I go back and find my grandparents, and go back and I find the Hasidim, and go back and find the Kabbalists, and I go back—memory must go back until it goes back to the source of memory. It is a creative channel.

P: Everything in Judaism says, "Remember."

EW: Absolutely. We have lived through such events.

P: In a certain way, my life is not only the events of my life. Isn't this something that has to be faced?

EW: Events are outside, reverberations inside. To be awake means to listen to these events. Each event is a code, history is telling us something, God is telling us something, and if we don't try to decode the message, then what will make us understand it?

The Indigenous Perspective

If One Thing
Stands, Another
Will Stand Beside It

CHINUA ACHEBE

Vol. 17, No. 3
"The Oral Tradition"

Giveaway for
the Gods

ARTHUR AMIOTTE

Vol. 15, No. 4
"Hospitality"

Why We're
Here Today

Singing the World

Moving Through
Milestones

CHIEF TOM PORTER

HEATHER VALENCIA

SOBONFU SOMÉ

**Vol. 24, No. 2
"Prayer & Meditation"**

**Vol. 25, No. 2
"Riddle & Mystery"**

**Vol. 25, No. 4
"Fate and Fortune"**

If One Thing Stands, Another Will Stand Beside It

An Interview with Chinua Achebe

From PARABOLA Vol. 17, No. 3, "The Oral Tradition"

> **Chinua Achebe,** the Nigerian novelist of Igbo tribal descent, has frequently used traditional folk tales as background in his novels, which include **Things Fall Apart** (Knopf) and **Anthills of the Savannah** (Anchor). He is Charles P. Stevenson Jr. Professor of Languages and Literature at Bard College.

PARABOLA: You once spoke of an incident when you and your wife were shopping in a supermarket in Nigeria and for the first time paid attention to the kind of Westernized children's books that were being sold there. It seemed that something really vital was being lost which had been present in your own past: storytelling in the home.

CHINUA ACHEBE: That was one of the most important learning experiences I had as a parent. It had not occurred to me that we were failing so badly in our responsibilities and that such a gap existed: our child was growing up without something of great value, the story. Children's storybooks were coming from abroad and we simply bagged them with our groceries and threw them to our children without bothering to find out what was inside them.

I don't mean the child had no stories at all, but we had not maintained the storytelling tradition as a conscious form of socialization, the way it was nightly in my childhood. And the kind of story that was read in day-care centers and kindergarten did not really fill this need, did not make up for the nightly storytelling sessions at home.

P: What were those storytelling sessions like when you were a child?

CA: We were told mostly animal stories, about the tortoise, the leopard, birds—all kinds of animals, all kinds of people. And you became so familiar with them, for you were not only told the stories: you were expected to tell them, you took turns. It was often the same story, over and over again. You acquired the ability to tell the stories. A child gets to know the story and doesn't really want it changed too much, fundamentally. You could alter it just a little bit—that introduces variety and amusement. But if you attempted to make it really different, the other children would object. They'd say, no, that's not the story!

It's difficult to explain what this does to the mind, but it's extremely important. The child becomes familiar with this whole world that is different from the everyday world—the world of the story—and begins to enjoy it and becomes part of it. And this is what I think our daughter was missing. Children need stories. It's not enough that they read them in books, or that books are read to them.

If you cannot have the nightly storytelling sessions because of the way we live these days, then books are better than nothing—I'm not underrating the importance of children's books. But I am saying that if children can have the sessions, the nightly sessions, they will much prefer that.

P: When you began to learn the stories and to tell them yourself, would the other children correct you, or would the adult correct you?

CA: If you didn't tell the story right, the other children would stop you. It was as if you didn't know anything if you got it wrong: it was really extraordinarily important to them. I was lucky to have my older sister, who could mimic the voice of the tortoise when he's doing something naughty, the way he would sound.

That was one kind of story. The other kind of story is the history of people. That's also important. The oral tradition is really a complex of everything—all the language arts, from fiction to history to politics.

P: Perhaps the oral tradition is not so easy to define as we think.

CA: Oh no, it's not. It's very big, because as I've indicated, everything that we as human beings have learned to talk about and discuss and reflect upon through language is part of this oral tradition: you have flippant talk, you have very serious discussion, you have history, you have religion, you have stories, fiction if you like—all that is part of it. But one thing which is common to all of that, I think, is the seriousness with which language has to be treated, if it is the only vehicle you have for conveying your meaning, for reflecting. I don't mean you can't play with language, but you need to know what you are doing, at all times. If a man is on the pulpit to preach, you don't expect him to start using flippant talk—that's not appropriate in the church. But when you are outdoors, playing with friends, you can talk and make fun of people and it won't necessarily offend.

So there are different registers for the use of language. What is appropriate in one situation may not be appropriate in another—you have to be conscious of that. And you have to make sure that this distinction is maintained between the serious and the unserious, between work and play, when language is the only thing you have to express yourself in a very complex and difficult world.

P: How does a child learn to make those distinctions?

CA: I think this is taught instinctively in the handling of stories. For instance, Tortoise is a trickster, and when he's saying one thing, you soon learn that he means something else. All the other creatures in the story know that Tortoise is not to be trusted. So you begin to draw this distinction between what is to be trusted or who is to be trusted, and what is not to be trusted. I think it is a slow and painless way of introducing the child to this, with different categories and registers of speech.

P: Could you give us an example of a Tortoise story?

CA: Let me give you one from *Things Fall Apart,* my novel, because I have often adapted material from the oral tradition into my writing.

There's a story about Tortoise and the birds. The birds are planning to go to the sky, because the people in the sky have invited them to a feast. So they are getting ready and there is a lot of excitement. And somehow Tortoise—who is very greedy, apart from being a trickster, and always manages to get to wherever anything is happening—finds out that something is cooking, and he visits the birds and asks them to take him along to the feast in the sky. But they all know Tortoise and they don't want to have anything to do with him. They say "No, no, we know you too well, Tortoise!" But Tortoise says "No, no, no, you don't know me. I've changed. I've become a totally different person, I am no longer the trickster you used to know. I'm now law-abiding." So he persuades them, because he's very smooth, very well-spoken. He even gets them to donate one feather each to build him a pair of wings so that he can fly to the sky with them.

Then, being Tortoise, he virtually takes over the expedition, and he tells the birds that it is customary to take new names when you are going on a big outing like this. They've never heard of this custom, but somehow they think, "Well, he's been everywhere, he's very well traveled, so he must know what he's talking about." So they begin to take praise names, like Daughter of Heaven, or Arrow that Shoots the Sky. And Tortoise then says "My own name is All of You," and they all laugh, and they say, "This is wonderful, we are very lucky to have such an amusing fellow with us."

They set out, Tortoise flying along with the birds, and when they get there, the people of the sky set this enormous feast before them, and Tortoise jumps up and says, "Who is this for?" And the sky people say "All of you!" And so Tortoise says, "Well, that's my name, so this is all for me!"

The birds, of course, are furious. In the end they get their revenge by taking back all their feathers from Tortoise. So he is stranded up there in the sky, high and dry! And the birds fly away, hungry and angry, but not before Tortoise has convinced them to carry a message to his wife, instructing her to bring out soft things and pile them in the compound, so that he can jump. The birds tell his wife to bring out all the hard stuff instead: wood and mortar and grinding stones. Tortoise sees people moving around down below, but he can't see what they are laying out. So in the end, when he thinks everything is ready, he lets go, and falls to his compound and smashes his shell completely. His friends go and get a famous physician, who fortunately is able to put the pieces of shell together again and glue them, which is why the shell of the tortoise is so uneven.

That's Tortoise—he's there in virtually every story. If you don't see Tortoise, you know that things haven't really got going.

P: So what does a story do in your tradition, or does it serve many purposes?

CA: It does many things. It entertains, it informs, it instructs. It is the most complete way of communicating. Tortoise is a character children can relate to. He is a rogue, but he's a nice kind of rogue. I think children don't trust him, but they like to hear that he's around, because they know that he's going to do something unexpected and generally he will be punished too. This is the moral side of it. He's not allowed to get away with murder. He does something and he is punished, but he still lives to appear again, so it's not cheap Sunday school morality that we're talking about; it is something that is even more interesting, I think. There is crime and punishment. It's not mechanical. Tortoise is wicked, but he is not irredeemably so. Tortoise is not evil. He's just naughty.

P: Do these stories present the concepts of the religion of the Igbo tribe? Is there a direct connection there?

CA: Everything is connected for the Igbo. I think the notion of compartments such as religion, politics, economics—these divisions do not operate in the traditional Igbo world view. If you ask an Igbo man what his religion is, he will be at a loss to answer you. Or if you ask him if he is religious, it's the same thing, because to him everybody—and everything—is religious. It's a holistic world view. Things are linked.

If you look at these stories carefully, you will find they support and reinforce the basic tenets of the culture. The storytellers worked out what is right and what is wrong, what is courageous and what is cowardly, and they translate this into stories. The Igbo society, for example, does not believe in the single-mindedness of some religions. The Igbo think that the world can be better explained in terms of not one thing, but always the other as well—they always look for the other. And they say it in so many different ways, but the most concise one, the most frequent is *"Ife kwulu, ife akwudebie* (If one thing stands, another thing will stand beside it)." Things don't come by themselves.

One of the most complete pictures of evil for the Igbo is Something That Doesn't Even Wear a Necklace. There is no second presence—not even a necklace—so this thing is so completely alone that it is a metaphor for evil: something that doesn't even have a necklace to keep it company.

This idea of the importance of the second occurs again and again and again. Another way they put it is, "Two heads, four eyes." They don't bother to tell you more than that: If you have two heads, you'll have four eyes. And four is an image of completeness to the Igbo. The four points of the compass, the four days of the Igbo week. You can see around the problem if you have four eyes. If you just have two eyes, one head, you can't see around the corner. And so they repeat this notion of the importance of many, rather than one.

P: Isn't this particularly true with stories, where you can have all sorts of characters, not only the hero, but the coward as well?

CA: Exactly. It makes it possible for you to avoid excess. The main character of *Things Fall Apart* believes in strength, in manliness, in working hard and providing for his family—unlike his father, who was a ne'er-do-well. And you think, OK, here is a man who deserves the approval of his people. This is true, but his people say there is also a danger in being strong and manly. They make a proverb: "We stand in the compound of a coward, and point to the ruins of the home of the strong man." The coward is alive; his compound is still there. But there are ruins where the courageous man used to live.

So Igbo thought is full of these reminders. They're not saying you should go and be a coward, they're saying, whatever you do remember the other possibility, the other side.

P: In *Things Fall Apart,* there was one place where something is said about the women telling one kind of stories and the men telling another kind. In our Western culture, with all the emphasis on equal rights, it's almost out of style for men to have one role and women to have another. Do you think these roles are important?

CA: I'm not the one to instruct you on what you should do in your own culture. All I can say is, this is one way of looking at the world. It has its merits and it no doubt has its defects. Whichever way we are adopting, whatever culture, it is good to know that the world is very big, and that there will be other ways if you travel far enough, and that the person who stays at home and says "Mine is the right one" is often most impoverished. Igbo people understand quite well that their way of looking at the world is not the only one, or should not be the only one. They say that a young man who has never traveled imagines that his mother makes the best soup in the world. So they encourage you to travel, with all respect to your mother.

P: Can you describe the difference between the kinds of stories that the men tell and those that the women tell?

CA: The basic difference is that men, once they've grown up, tell historical stories, more about how the town came into existence, the history, the various families, how they relate to one another. That's their domain. This is something very complex and important for the life of the community. My father, who was a Christian convert and a teacher, had pretty much abandoned the traditional life of the Igbo society, but he was still so imbued with this aspect of the life of the community that before he died he dictated to my brother the entire genealogy of our town, from the man who was the first ancestor down to every family, and my brother got this down on paper. I saw that happen. Unfortunately it was lost during the Biafran war.

That's the kind of instruction that men were given, the kind of education they were given. You knew exactly how every part of the town fit into the family tree. Then if there was a land quarrel between families, or between sections of the town, you would ask the oldest people. That was their job; they would know. And they would not play any tricks about this—it was a sacred duty.

And the fact that they would be called upon once in a while to make this kind of declaration kept them active in mind and memory. They really do remember. They remember much better than we do, those of us who write things down. Because once you transfer everything to a notebook, you don't have to remember it anymore—the notebook remembers for you. For the Igbo, it's not like that—they have to keep remembering. I have seen some very, very old people, and it's rare to find an old man who has lost his mind because he doesn't use it. I don't remember senility among the Igbo. It is something which is yet to come to us, with literacy and writing.

P: And the women's stories?

CA: The women's stories are mostly the usual folktale kind of story. It doesn't mean the women don't know the history; they do—they know some of it. The position of the woman is that she generally comes from another clan, because you have to go outside the group to marry. And so the woman, coming from there, is not really in a position to know as much about here as the man is. This is a fact. And so her position is therefore different.

This is why when I talk about separating people by gender, there are certain areas where the very nature of the woman makes it inevitable that her role will be different. Not inferior—it shouldn't be inferior—but different. Igbo people tend to look at the woman more as an ambassador: she's from somewhere else; she's here, as it were, on duty. Her rights and privileges at home are not damaged by the fact that she's married here. She's still there as one of the daughters of her original home, and in fact when she dies she is taken back there and buried—she is not buried in her husband's village. You have to take her back. The role of the woman is very interesting, and very complex in this kind of society.

P: So the women that come to the village will come from other places. Will their folklore be different? Will they bring different versions of the stories?

CA: It depends on how far. My mother, for instance, came from twenty miles away, which was a long distance in those days! That's where my wife comes from, too. Their stories will be somewhat different, but not very different. But if you were to go a hundred miles or two hundred miles away, then you might begin to have different versions, but still variations on the same themes.

P: So they'd be confronting each other, in a way. But isn't this simply another example of: "If one thing stands, another will stand beside it"?

CA: Yes, the differences are highly admired, they are not put down.

P: Are there *griots,* or singing storytellers, among the Igbo, as there are among other West African tribes?

CA: There are. In a way, there shouldn't be, I suppose, because we tend to think of griots as professional storytellers in hierarchical societies, with kings and nobility. The Igbo long ago abandoned the notion of kingship, in favor of an egalitarian system of government. They know about kings, from neighboring tribes like the Benin and the Yoruba, but they have deliberately chosen not to have them.

P: Aren't griots usually praise singers, official bards who flatter the kings and other political figures in public?

CA: Yes, that's what they do normally. Therefore by rights, there should not be any griots among the Igbo, because the Igbo are very democratic. Everybody is a priest of sorts, and everybody is a historian, everybody's a storyteller.

But there are also epic traditions in some parts of Igboland, and epic storytellers and poets do this not as their only way of life, but as a good part of their occupation. In the season after the harvest, there will be storytelling competitions among these professional storytellers, and they tell of heroes who fought against monsters and against all kinds of oppressors—including one, which I like very much, about an oppressor who had moved his house to the heavens, and from there was throwing down commandments.

According to this story, the whole village was flooded with paper falling down from the sky. People would pick up this paper, and those who could read would read and then start crying, and those who could not read would take the paper to someone who could read and have it read to them, and they would all burst out crying. And eventually it turns out that this is a commandment from this man in the sky, ordering the entire community to fast for seven weeks. And seven weeks means twenty-eight days, since in Igbo society there are four days to the week. So that meant one month, with no food, no water—nothing at all should pass between their lips for these twenty-eight days. Why? Because this person in the sky is having a feast and to honor his feast the people down here must go without any nourishment!

So all the famous heroes in Igboland assemble, and they set out to discover why this should be so. But to find the road to the sky is virtually impossible. So in the end, everybody turns back, after many days and weeks of struggling on the way to the sky, and only one man, a hero named Emeka Okoye, and his praise-singer, who is a wildcat, make it there—and carry the tyrant bodily back to earth.

So these traditional griots and poets are not only telling old stories, but they also add and subtract, and this is the way it's always been. I invited some of them to the university to recite for the university community, and it was very interesting the little changes that I noticed between what they said back in their villages and what they said at the university. Nothing was radically different, but they knew that this was a different kind of society. The images changed sometimes. They would talk about distances now as between here and Lagos [the capital of Nigeria], because they knew these are people who would know about Lagos. In the villages you would not expect people to be able to gauge distances or the size of forests stretching "from here to Lagos."

These are the things which the oral tradition does automatically—which makes it difficult for purists to deal with it. They would prefer that these traditions not change at all, but the makers don't think that way. They make what they regard as enough changes so that what they are saying or doing can be relevant or important to their audience.

P: So the oral tradition can survive the transition from village to city life?

CA: It is very difficult to move it in the same form. That's what I meant when I said that if we find we can no longer maintain the environment for storytelling—with people leaving, going to school, moving out of the villages into the towns—then the best we can do is to try and translate some of the energy of the folk stories into the written stories.

P: What is the relationship between traditional stories and fiction?

CA: They will never be the same. They don't have to be exactly the same. But it will be very valuable if we can develop a literary tradition that carries the intonations of this great past.

P: Is this what made you decide to become a writer?

CA: It was one of the reasons, I'm sure. I didn't think of it that way at the time. The decision to become a writer is not something you make so consciously as that. I was just excited by stories. That's a good enough reason.

But there were other reasons, including the fact that I had not seen myself or my people in the stories or novels I was reading. It was the same with the children's stories that we bought for my daughter, which I mentioned earlier.

There are so many things we have to do all at once today, because the world is changing so fast around us, and a lot of it we are not in control of, but what we do control I think we should think about seriously. This is especially true with story, because that's really the basis of our existence—who we are, what we think we are, what our people say we are, what other people think we are—all of this is very important. And sometimes what is inside stories is straightforward poison.

P: The poison that's in some stories, should it be somehow forbidden—censored in some way—or should it simply be countered with another story?

CA: Countering it with another story is my way. I don't think anything should be forbidden. Trying to legislate stories out of existence is a sign of weakness, and it really doesn't work anyway. Where one story stands, bring another one to stand beside it, and if that's a better story, then it should displace the bad one. I think that's the way it should be. If, on the other hand, it is necessary to have the two of them side by side, then you don't lose anything.

There are so many people today whose stories need to be told—Africans, Native Americans, women everywhere—no story should be banned. It can be discussed and even interrogated, but that should not diminish whatever value the story has. Rather it puts each story in a proper perspective, and it will also encourage diversity. Those who have not spoken so far need to be heard, all around the world. And we will not be poorer, we will be richer for that.

Giveaway for the Gods

An Interview with Arthur Amiotte

From PARABOLA Vol. 15, No. 4, "Hospitality"

Arthur Amiotte, well-known Lakota artist, author, and educator, has been a friend of **PARABOLA** since 1976, when the account of his first vision quest appeared in our third issue. He was involved with the establishment of the Museum of the American Indian in New York City and Washington D. C. under the auspices of the Smithsonian Institution.

PARABOLA: To begin with, would you explain what a Sioux giveaway is, and how it relates to the idea of an exchange between people or levels which constitutes hospitality?

ARTHUR AMIOTTE: A giveaway is a ceremony among our people where one family invites a lot of people to attend a gathering and great quantities of goods and foodstuffs are distributed to the guests. There are many stories from our mythology that speak to us of times and places when gods and human beings and animals were interacting with each other in the sacred world. The idea of a feast taking place at which the gods and the humans and other beings were gathered seems central to all these occasions, wherein people come together and "share" in something—the idea  of people gathered in a circle, with food being distributed. Our mythology tells us that when humans lived beneath the earth, they raised a particular kind of white fruit (they were vegetarians, and they would not eat meat). It was their role to be servants to the gods—the Sun, the Moon, the creator gods, and the secondary gods—and to give them this fruit when they gathered at these occasions. So one might say that the distribution of food is a means of connectedness between sacred principles and what we are as human beings. It is a reciprocal kind of activity in which we are reminded of sacred principles. Indeed the very ceremonies which have come down to us all include the distribution of food either before or after or during the rite itself.

P: The idea really is, then, that it is the gods who are fed—the feast is for the gods. Therefore is the giveaway a three-way exchange, between the giver, and the recipients, and the gods?

AA: Yes, it does go beyond just the food. One prime example of this is during the child sanctification rite. A central part of the ceremony is the giving away of food and goods. The family who is sponsoring the ceremony wish to sanctify their child, honor that child, by reminding it and blessing it in the ways of the sacred; they are essentially saying, "We love this child so much that we wish to honor other human beings." So they take on another couple as godparents or surrogate parents for this child in a ritual adoption. Central to the rite is a time when food is placed at the child's lips, and the people who are to be adopted say, "I'm hungry." The food then is taken away from the child and given to them. Water is given to the child, and the adoptees say, "I am thirsty," so the water is taken from the child and given to them. Then goods, decorated garments and robes—in modern times, blankets—are placed on the back of the child, but then the surrogate parents say, "I am cold," and the robes are placed instead on their backs. Then the surrogate parents say, "You have done as a good *hunka,* a beloved one, should do. You have taken food from yourself and given it to someone who is hungry, you have taken water from yourself and given it to someone who is thirsty, you have taken the clothes from your back and given it to someone who is cold. This is the way it should always be. Should you always do this then you shall live a long life, and you will be blessed with many children, and many good things will happen to you if you follow these principles. Even if a poor dog should come to your door and you have the last bit of food in your mouth, at least take out half of it and give it to this animal. Even if you do not have anything to eat and visitors come to your house, at least give them water. If you should remember to do all these things, much goodness will come to you in life, you will be a fortunate person, you will be blessed, you will have all that you need. If ever you should forget this, then all of your blessings will be as ashes in your mouth."

In fact, the hunka children and those families who sponsor them take a lifelong vow to be of perpetual assistance. It becomes their mission in life to provide the necessities so that orphans and poor people can continually come to their homes. When visitors come to the house, a young girl is expected to serve food to them, a young man is expected to help serve food and take care of their needs. On the contemporary reservation, a trunk is purchased for girls who have been through this ceremony. The girls have been taught to do beading and quilling as early as possible, and they are to put this handwork in the trunk. When visitors come, or when elderly people come that they have not seen in a long time, all the mother has to do is give the girl a nod and the girl goes and opens her trunk and takes out scarves or pieces of calico and gives them to these guests. This is the means of training the girls in this process. The young men, when they made their first kill, were expected to cut up the animal and take parts of it and give it to the needy and the elderly in the community.

P: Is there a belief that the gods are also fed by this? I am putting this in a very literal way, but we have to understand the meaning behind it.

AA: Yes. But usually the foods and the goods are purified and sanctified, the belief being that the spirit-like selves of these objects do indeed go to the gods first. That is why the offering is usually placed on the ground, it is prayed over, it is purified with the smoke of sweetgrass, and in a sense the essence of these things becomes first of all the gift to the gods. The humans participate—but it is like eating oranges after all the juice has been squeezed out, eating the peelings, as it were.

P: If the gods receive the essence, the juice, and the people receive the orange peels, the goods; what about the giver? Is it a step towards his own transformation?

AA: For the giver, the greatest part of the transformation is sacrifice, to give away these wonderful things, as opposed to hoarding them. It eventually works within one's mind that potentially, as Ella Deloria says (in *Speaking of Indians*, which was a 1940 publication), "things are made to be given." In time, things will come back to you, yes. And there is a standard of quality that says: Never give anything away that is less in quality and beauty than what you yourself would be proud to own.

P: What is the cultural origin of the giveaway?

AA: Historically it was the transformation from an Eastern Plains, semi-sedentary group of people to a nomadic hunting group. It became necessary to modify their lifestyle by owning fewer and fewer possessions, because they had to move about. Prairie fires, tornadoes, enemies, the hunt—they had to be able to pick up and move as rapidly as possible. So it became common for people to own very few things. The things they did own were transportable, unbreakable, and many times were the only sources available for decoration. Some of the ceremonial garb and the interiors of the tipis were well decorated, because there was a second element at work, which was the admonition to be industrious, not to be lazy. This meant that everyone, particularly women and young girls, were continually making things. They could not keep them, so according to the sacred principle of helping the less fortunate, they were given to the orphans and the elderly, so that everyone within the band would be taken care of. So the idea was to make things that were beautiful, to concentrate on technique. They would have women's feasts when the women would get together and display the things that they had made, when actually there would be a competition and the elder craftswomen would judge these things.

The idea was that you ennobled the object itself, and others within the group, by giving them these fine things. One of the worst kinds of insults was to pretend to retain possession over these things that you had made and given away. The admonition is that if you think you own these goods even though they belong to someone else, you must cut yourself off from them and think in another way.

P: When is a giveaway ceremony done?

AA: There are numerous occasions connected with the giveaway. The feast and the giveaway actually accompany all major ceremonies. They are an integral part of them. They become like one of the offerings that is made to the gods and to the people on all these occasions.

P: Does it accompany the Sun Dance?

AA: Yes. There are feasts before, during, and after. The dancers do not eat this food, except at the first one and the last one. But in between, there are numerous occasions. People are naming their children, and will have a naming feast for their child. That would be accompanied by a feast and a giving away of gifts. There are also the hunka, or the young woman's ceremony, or the children's throwing the ball ceremony. Some people have a sweat lodge near their homes, and when they have a ceremony, an important part of it is that when it is over, a meal is served, maybe not very much, but those who sponsor it will provide those who have participated in their sweat ceremony with a meal afterwards.

P: Is the giveaway ever a ceremony by itself?

AA: No, not by itself. Let me carry it one step further, into death. Upon the death of a person, in the Sioux tradition, there is a meal provided after the burial. If the family has goods on hand or can get goods, they will have a giveaway at that time. Things will be given to the pall bearers, to the people who have come and attended the wake, to people who have brought food or flowers, to friends of the deceased; in some cases the clergy, if they are invited, will receive things—it's a way of reciprocating. Then, usually a year following that, during a memorial feast, in what was traditionally the old spirit-keeping ceremony, another, larger feast and giveaway is held to honor the deceased, at which time members of the community and visitors from great distances and people who are significant in the life of the deceased or the family will receive things. Then there are other occasions; four days or a week or a month after the death, people who are not in mourning gather things up to take to the mourners and have a mourners' feast, where the relatives of the deceased are actually fed the good things that have been brought. And because they have given away all their worldly goods, dishes, new pots and pans, things of this nature are given to them.

P: At other kinds of giveaways, what criteria are there for determining who receives goods? Are the people who come to a giveaway ceremony all invited guests or friends?

AA: There are three levels of giving away. The first one, which is considered to be the least important, is *Otunhanpi*. That is when an individual person is recognized by being called up in front of the group and is given goods. At that time it is appropriate to shake hands or embrace the family who are giving you these things, and the person in whose honor it is being given. Otunhanpi implies an individual relationship between that person and the person being honored or the family. It can mean that at some time in the past, this person has been of great help to the family, and that their status and their knowledge and their wisdom are very special, that the traits this person exhibits are what the family is celebrating at this time. For some groups, not so much the Sioux, but many of the Plains groups, it also implies a reciprocal arrangement. There are some who would say that some of the people who are called up are expected at some time in the future to return something. There are people who will call up someone who they know is getting ready to give something away in the next month or so, with the hope of being called up at their give-away. So the Trickster still reigns in all of these kinds of transactions!

In this first kind of giving away, in many cases it is customary to honor people who are of fine character, of integrity and grace. That's why on occasion the elderly people who are called up were hunka people when they were young, they have given away all of their life, they are known in every community. So, whether you know them or not, if they are known to be of this kind of people who welcome people to their home, who share with them, who raise their grandchildren, who sacrifice for the benefit of others, on these occasions they are called up and honored individually, simply because they belong to that society of people who do that intentionally.

The second kind of giving away is what is known as *ohunkesni*—"the pitiful, the helpless, the needy." This consists of picking up the goods and passing them around, indiscriminately, to the people who are there, and you keep on doing that until everything is gone. Each person takes what he is given. We make it a practice in our part of the country to give away fine things—Pendleton blankets or jackets, quilts, hand towels, scarves, yardage of cloth, dishes, enamel or plastic ware—and we hand out these things, as well as giving them to the people we call up. The ohunkesni form is the equal distribution of goods. That implies no obligation whatsoever between the receiver and the giver.

The third kind is known as *wihpeyapi,* and that literally means "throwing away." In other words, the goods are simply spread out all over the ground, and whoever wants or needs them can go up and get them, and the givers just stand back (and suffer!). This form is considered the ultimate form, the greatest and most sacred form of sacrifice, because you are above these "things," you are concerned with another realm. The idea is that well-behaved people, well-behaved receivers, will go and choose something, maybe one or two things, so that the next person will have something to take. But there are occasions when there are greedy people who go and just grab armfuls and armfuls and retreat, and do not leave anything for the remainder of the people. So this kind of giving away implies the greater sacrifice, but it also expects a responsibility on the part of the receivers that they will conduct themselves modestly. There are occasions when the givers will tell certain people to go get what they want. That is always very embarrassing, because if you go and you're really humble and take the smallest thing there, the giver will be insulted. But then if you pick too much, this would insult the giver as well! Usually the way we handle this is to make piles: a Pendleton, a shawl—it becomes a unit, and that is what they are expected to take.

The last form is most significant, because that is what was usually done at funerals. There was a time when, after the funeral, people were allowed to walk into the house and take whatever they wanted of the household goods, the furniture, the linens, the clothing, until the family was reduced to absolutely nothing. Originally, they gave away their entire tipi and all their worldly goods. But in those days, four days later, the people would probably bring you a new tent and new garments—not always. At that time, that kind of sacrifice could be done, as a total giving over, as it were, to the mourning process, to the loss of this beloved one, making oneself miserable and near death as well, as it was also a practice to gash their legs and cut their arms. It was this kind of activity that caused the prohibition of these kinds of ceremonies in the early days on the reservations.

P: So people were sometimes left then, with nothing? They were not taken care of?

AA: That's right. The idea was that if you were a responsible neighbor, a responsible relative, you would see to it that they were restored to a modicum of wealth to continue their lives.

P: That is following a death, a funeral ceremony. In the other kinds of giveaways, is there any kind of measure of how much you give away, to what extent you impoverish yourself?

AA: Yes. It has to do with your collective family wealth. How much you have, and the quality of the goods. In other words, if you are following the old admonition to never give away anything less in value or quality than what you yourself would be proud to own, that implies then that the things you give away are very fine if you have high standards. Then you only give away fine things, which can put a strain on you, especially if you are an artist, or if your family are craftsmen! There are other people who will make shoddy goods, to accumulate a great quantity. The quantity and the quality are usually determined by the individuals doing it, and their standard of living. For example, there are some very poor people who insist on doing this but they really can't afford to have the quilts quilted, so they will tack them, tie them. Then there are those who cannot even afford the batting and the undersides, so they only make and give away the tops. Sometimes the tops are made from variegated materials, they are not color coordinated or matched.

P: When you speak of a "family," what is the scope of that?

AA: We are talking about an extended family who have several generations— the grandparents, possibly numerous aunts and uncles, cousins, the biological parents, or adoptive parents, the siblings—all contributing things that they have made or money to purchase materials to have other people make these things.

P: Is there one person at the center of each family? How are decisions made?

AA: The decision can be made by "the elders"—for example, in my own family, my grandmother was the matriarch, and she often decided things. And then as I grew to maturity, I became the head man, and my mother and aunts were willing to participate, because it brought them status, and now with the passing of my grandmother, that power rests in the hands of three of my women relatives—my mother and my two aunts are the ones who have done these traditional kinds of activities, they are the ones who now decide which names will be given, and when these good things will take place.

P: It sounds as if there is a certain fluidity of roles. If a giveaway is in the context of a larger ceremony, then the roles are always changing. You will be the sponsor of a Sun Dance, but during that time, someone else might decide to hold a giveaway. So the roles of host and the guest are constantly shifting.

AA: Yes. I was thinking about that this morning. Over the years, in going to these different places, it is not enough for us to go as "house guests," and expect to be fed and housed and taken care of. We have this tribal or group identity. When I moved to Standing Rock and was asked to help sponsor the Sun Dance, and then on up to Manitoba, and eventually was a major partici- pant, it was not enough for me to go as an intercessor and expect to be taken care of. My Lakota identity requires that I reciprocate, out of not "me" but out of my people's identity. I had to take my group of people with me. Hence our encampment, made up of relatives—we had to have "our own home" where I could reciprocate properly to these people who had invited me. I sup- pose it is comparable to a house guest bringing some of his own food. And then you also give things to the host. Within our own camp, we had to be able to offer hospitality while we were in a foreign country—while we were guests, we also had to practice hospitality, and reciprocate to our hosts.

I am inclined to think that Lakota hospitality is closely tied in with a group identity and group mentality and group ethos, because these things are done as a group. There is a very old ceremony done on the Plains: When two Sioux groups would meet on the Plains—they might be northern Sioux and Oglalas travelling—whenever they would meet, the group that knew that it was well supplied and could do it would appear on the prairie, and they would all sit down on their haunches, and the other group, if it were willing to accept this group's hospitality, would advance singing honoring songs toward the group that was sitting, holding their hands out toward them. In other words, it was the reversal of what you would expect guest and host to do. Then they would set up their camp together, and the ones that were squatting would host the ones who came forward singing to them.

Moving into modern times, we have nuclear families who live in single family households, but the element of hospitality can exist in any variety of ways. If one is abiding by the traditions, it is customary, when people arrive in a Lakota home, to immediately offer them something to drink or something to eat, and to give them a nice place to sit, and then possibly also to give gifts to them when they leave. So you may be practicing a Lakota version of hospitality, but you might be offering Belgian chocolates or espresso coffee.

P: What is the proper way for the guest to receive hospitality?

AA: To receive it with grace, fully realizing that he is being honored, and that at some time in the future, should it occur, he will reciprocate in like manner. It makes the giver feel very good, when people are travelling or coming from a great distance and are operating at a minimum level, to take care of their needs. When guests come, you serve them the best that you have, and you look after them, and the expectation is that they will be pleased, that they will be honored to be a guest in your home. If they are of a special relationship, then you also give them things when they leave, to ease their journey and make them feel good, because they are away from their group. And if they are your people, or your kind of people, then for a moment that places a reminder of who they are and where they've come from, the kind of people they belong to.

P: What we have been beginning to see in the idea of hospitality is that there is an exchange between two forces: the force that must be there and the force that must move. Where that is lacking or becomes artificial, everything seems to go astray. There isn't any real exchange except between these two; they absolutely have to have each other, they must exchange, for their own lives.

AA: There is also a recognition of an ultimate possibility that your situation might change—that whole possibility of loss and decline, the whole idea of losing the family wealth. If you should not have any food, at least you can give the visitor water. The focusing in on the ultimate need of people to meet and care for each other. Out of that comes all the etiquette, where you should sit in the tipi and how to behave.

P: There is a different angle that comes in with the expectation of a return. For instance, in accounts of the West Coast potlatch, it seems this is done for the purpose of increasing one's wealth, because other people must, in honor, pay you back even more than you have given them.

AA: That is true about the Northwest Coast people and the meaning of pot-latch, which the Sioux people and the Plains tribes do not subscribe to. It is a unique system of a people who live sedentarily in a place for a long time wherein there is great wealth—the sea and the land there are very rich and gave them a lot. There was a great deal of trade, and there was a great influx of non-Indian goods. They had this state system, their tribal chiefs were almost like kings. They had absolute control over their units, their clans—they actually owned slaves. In the Northwest there was also the concept of interest: I give this thing to you now, and in time it's going to grow into four of these, and because of my status as chief, when it comes time I deserve four of these back. And there was the system of coppers—copper plaques repre-senting so much wealth. All these concepts are built on this whole abstrac-tion of interest.

P: Because of the way they lived, they never had to experience the role of the one who travels, the guest; they were always the host.

AA: Sometimes they would play host to other villages, but there was a sense of "I am the host and I am going to outdo you." When this other group went home and decided that they could outdo the other village, then they would invite them.

P: But that was a sort of artificial recreation of the traveler. The traveler wasn't travelling because of any need of his own, he was travelling because someone important said, "You come here." And then he went back and stayed in the same place he had come from, whereas in the nomadic tradition of the Plains, people would not necessarily go back to the same place.

AA: The Northwest tradition is very foreign to the idea of the giveaway that I am talking about. Some of the Plains groups have this element of "tit for tat," but possibly because they could not carry around all this stuff on the Plains with them, they had to accommodate to the concept of sacrifice, total release and transcendence over this kind of materialism. In exchange, your status grew in the eyes of the people, and you became a much respected person by how much you gave away, not by how much you had: by the number of cer-emonies you performed, the number of giveaways your family had. So the Plains giveaway is an acceptance of the transitory nature of materialism, that it's not *things* that really count, even though you work very hard creating and accumulating them. The idea is that you are a much finer and greater person by not having a great deal of wealth, and by being able to utilize what you have as a means for ennobling the human spirit. When you give, it becomes an act of love; you think more of these people than you do of these goods, you think more of their particular needs, or what these gifts symbolize. The robe, the blanket, and the shawl symbolize warmth; no one should be cold. Food is the same way; no one should be hungry. These objects and the food become symbolic of the basic needs that people have. When you give away food, or pots and pans, you are saying, "I love you, the people, or you my tribe, or you my visitor, more than I love having these things or the money or the power that it takes to have and keep these things. So I am giving them to you now, and I expect nothing in return."

P: I have a very strong impression of the sense of community and of the need to make sacrifices for the community among your people—and as you said earlier, that this group ethos is the basis of your sense of hospitality. I think that connects with another understanding that the Native American has, that the adopted American does not: that we are all guests of the Earth, that it owns us, we don't own it. The white concept is that I own this piece of land, I have a deed to it, I put a fence around it. And Native Americans are being forced into that kind of attitude, by living in a society where it is the accepted and unquestioned way of living.

What do you think about the young people, and the possibility of the preservation of these traditional values, these traditional understandings of hospitality among your people?

AA: I don't know about the future of this. There are some dire things happening on my home reservation and on many other reservations, so I am not sure. There is great poverty and there are serious kinds of medical conditions, all of which will affect the future generations.

P: How many of them still have their language?

AA: Probably about forty to fifty percent still speak their language. But you have to remember that seventy-five percent of the reservation population is under the age of eighteen, on just about every reservation. It is usually the older generation of people who are carrying on these traditions. These eighteen-year-olds have to come into their maturity before they start doing these things.

P: You said earlier that the essence of the gifts given were for the gods. Is that something that is generally understood?

AA: No, that understanding exists only on an esoteric level. For instance, an honoring song: when the person is being honored, the music is primal, it's primordial, it's the ultimate recognition of the person for having sacrificed, and it's almost to the point where it's unexplainable, it reaches far into one's psyche, far into one's innermost self. This feeling becomes the reward for having done these things: the intensity of the moment of that song which recognizes this transcendence, that you have done something spiritual and good, not explained in terms of the way I have explained it—orange peelings, the juice, the gods.

P: Are those songs passed on, so that some kind of knowledge can continue to exist in the music itself?

AA: Yes.

P: And it exists in the language itself. That's why the language is so important, because behind the words there is a hidden meaning, so that even if people only learn the outer form of the words, the real meaning is there, and it's being preserved somehow.

AA: Lakota music is not one of those forms that has crossed over to be totally appreciated by non-Indian audiences. It is certainly appreciated by Indian people as sacredness and art. It's one of those things that a non-Indian would perhaps never understand. Inherent in those sounds are the principles that we are, on some level of our comprehension, moved by and aware of, in terms of the gods.

P: Is there anything in the language that expresses "please" and "thank you"?

AA: There are three forms for "thank you." For a common, courteous thank you, a man would say *pilamayelo*, a woman would say *pilamaye*. When you are very grateful, it's *wopila tanka*. And there is a silent form of thanking, which is to go like this (*he moves his hand, as if stroking the air in front of the interviewer's face*), which means "I am so grateful, I am stroking your face." That is the greatest form of "thank you."

P: There is a Lakota phrase that seems almost a "please" and a "thank you" at the same time: *Mitakuye oyasin*—"All my relatives."

AA: It's a single prayer by itself, if there is a group having a ceremonial gathering, whether it is a sweat lodge or a night ceremony; but it also comes at the end of most prayers. Mitakuye oyasin: "All my relatives—I am related to all." It's a closure, a recognition of relationship.

Why We're Here Today

An Interview with Chief Tom Porter

From PARABOLA Vol. 24, No. 2, "Prayer & Meditation"

Tom Porter is a highly respected Mohawk traditionalist whose lifelong commitment to the preservation and sharing of Mohawk language and culture led him to found a new community named **Kanatsiohareke** (The Place of the Clean Pot) on the site of an ancient Mohawk village near Fonda, New York.

Joseph Bruchac is an author and storyteller of Abenaki ancestry who lives in the Adirondack region of upstate New York. Author of more than one hundred books for adults and children, his works include his autobiography **Bowman's Store** (Lee & Low Books), **Skeleton Man** (HarperCollins), and **Trails of Tears, Paths of Beauty** (National Geographic Society Books).

JOSEPH BRUCHAC: Tom, for many people you're respected as one who cares about the spiritual side of life and the way that we're connected to all things and creation. I wanted to ask you, with that in mind, what is the purpose that prayer serves?

TOM PORTER: Well, I wasn't trained to read books. But one time I picked up a book by a Lakota man, *Fool's Crow*. He's talking about healers. When you heal, you have to make a prayer first. Some people thought that he was a good healer, but he said he was not the healer; it was God, the Creator. All he was is an air pipe. The Creator's spirit goes through this pipe and into whoever needs healing. Our job is to use prayer to keep the air pipe open and clean so the spirit can pass at will to do the job of healing and make a spiritual good life.

I liked that, and I thought it was a really good description; in fact, I immediately felt good about it. So that's what I call prayer. That's what prayer is for: to keep communication going in a spiritual world. I taught my kids since they were little babies how to pray. If you do that you're always aware—you can see good, and you can hear good too. You can see its beauty, and you can see everything there. That's what prayer does.

JB: Is prayer a way of making that connection that we have all around us, if not visible then tangible? We sense and connect to it through prayer. By giving breath to prayer we connect to the world.

TP: Yeah. If you don't, you become numb, callused. You don't really see and hear what you're supposed to: the birds singing, how beautiful it is. You don't enjoy the winter and the spring, the rain and the fog, and the days of sunshine.

JB: In some cultures, prayer is a way of asking for things. Do you see prayer that way?

JB: No. No, to the contrary. We rarely ever ask anything, because we don't have to. Everything's already here. The world is right here with us. All we have to do is say thank you. The Iroquois people's prayer is mostly "Thank you, thank you, thank you...." If you say "Thank you," once in a while, then those things that gave you your gifts, be it the earth, be it the sun, or thunder... well, then probably tomorrow they'll be happy to come back.

JB: So even something like, say, a lacrosse game could be a prayer. Anything we do can be a prayer, taking the Creator into creation.

TP: Thanking the Creator for the enjoyment of lacrosse, and its power to heal people.

JB: One thing you mentioned is the number of times traditional people would pray in the old days. What were you saying about that?

TP: Let me see if I can run through it the way it was told to us in our longhouse. As soon as you get up in the morning, even before you get out of bed, you see the light from the sun coming in the window. The first thing I say is, "You who are my Creator, I give you thankfulness and my greetings, my hello, and also my love." That's a prayer. As soon as you see the light, before you even get out of bed, that's how it begins.

Then, after greeting the Creator, you say, "My older brother, who is the sun, I who am the younger brother, give you greetings, too, and hello." That's already two. Then you get up and dress yourself, and you come down, and you see your mother or your father and you say to them, "Greetings and hello," and you give your love to your mother and father. Whenever you say "Hi," to someone, we consider that prayer, too. Everybody is a part of the Creator. That's why you're supposed to be nice to the animals, and to other human beings—and you're supposed to be nice to yourself, too, because the Creator is in your body as well. Every time you see somebody, say "hello" to them. Never forget this, because you are in fact saying hello to the Creator.

After you greet your family, you eat. When you finish your food, you say, "Niawen," and that is a prayer; it means "thank you," first to Creator—you said it only once, but the Creator hears it first—and then whoever fixed the food hears it second. The spirit of the food is the third one—or they hear it simultaneously, however it works. When you're in a real traditional long-house people's house, or if you go to a big meeting, you hear that all the time: Niawen. That's prayer for the food. It's not like Europeans; they have blessings for the food, but we Iroquois think the food is already blessed by the Creator in the beginning of the world. That's why it makes seeds. Every time we eat, that's a prayer.

You finish your food, you drink water. The minute you drink water, you say, "Niawen Shonkwaiàtíson." That means, "Thank you, my Creator," and "I give my hello, my greetings, my love, to the spirit of water." You can do it before, you can do it after; usually it's after. However many times you drink water in one day, you pray that many times. When you go swimming in a river, you never jump in that river before you first talk to it, and that's another prayer. So you say, "I give you my love, my hello, and my greetings," to the water spirit. That way, when you jump into the water it doesn't get scared, startled, or cause you to drown. That shows your respect for the river and the power that it stands for. You also have to acknowledge the spirit of that river or creek if you're passing over a bridge. As you're going over you say, "I'm crossing, I give you my greetings," so the water spirits don't bother you. If you go by without acknowledging them, they can make you depressed and lonesome. Even kids—if they cry and nobody knows why, well, maybe it's because they crossed that river and didn't pay respects by prayer.

When you go outside, the fresh morning air touches your face. Again you say, "Four sacred winds, my love to you, my thankfulness and my hello to you this morning as I felt you touch me, the fresh air touches my body. So I give you my greetings." That's to the four winds and to the Creator. I usually walk in the morning, a couple of miles, and when I see the grass I say "hello." That's prayer. I see the woods, trees, I say "hello." I see the birds, I say "hello."

When you see the actual sun, too, you stop and say again: "My Creator, thank you. Brother Sun, I thank you." Even though you said it earlier, you hadn't seen him directly, only his light. When you see his face, acknowledge again. Whatever you're doing that morning—even if you go to the barn to see the horses, you say "hello," to them, too. That's prayer, too. You're supposed to talk to the animals: "How are you doing? You doing okay?" If you have a dog or a cat, you say "hello," to them, too; and that's a prayer.

Say you're working in a garden. You're never supposed to go in a garden when you're angry or frustrated. You have to be happy and have a good mind in a garden. You talk to the corn and the beans, the potatoes or watermelon or strawberries, and you say "hello" to them. You say, "I come to clean your bed, where you live, to take the grass out so you can grow," and that's a prayer again. As you work, the sun is walking—that's what they call the sun's movements in the sky. When it reaches the middle of the sky, you stop what you're doing right there and you say to the sun, "My Creator, thank you again for sending my love. Real high in the sky, right in the middle of the universe, where you are, I thank you again, my older brother. Thank you for shining light. Thank you for bringing the energies and power I need to live." The sun goes by, and just before he goes over the horizon in the west, you stop again and you give greetings again for the day, all the day. You say, "Thank you for this day, all the miracles you've made. I hope I see you tomorrow." That's prayer.

These are examples of the way the Iroquois pray. If you go to a big mountain, you pray, too. If you see a big tree, you pray. And then when the sun has gone down and you're ready to go to bed, you say, "Creator, I give you my love again, and my greetings. I had a wonderful day today—I was working, I was healthy, everything was good, I got lots of things done. I didn't finish everything; maybe tomorrow I can finish, or the next day. So, Creator, I sleep tonight now, I give you my gratefulness for this past day. Hopefully, I will go peacefully through this night, and I will have the good fortune, with your power, to open my eyes to another miraculous day tomorrow." That's the way I was told by my elders.

Then there's the prayer of opening. That takes about an hour, or an hour and a half, the old way. I can still do it like that, but today everybody's in a hurry, so as soon as you start, everyone's looking at their clocks. (laugh) The old people didn't do that.

JB: The traditional opening prayer, which begins . . . how does it begin? With the earth itself?

TP: No, it begins with the Creator. Then the people, then the Mother Earth, and it goes up. . . .

JB: It works all the way through creation. How did the form of that prayer come to be?

TP: When the world, the creation, was made, that's where it came from. In the story of creation that prayer is built. It's the first thing we were given, to live on this earth, this thanksgiving.

JB: How does laughter relate to the sacred and to prayer?

TP: It's medicine. It can also be a diversion, but mostly it's a healing agent, a healing mechanism. You can make fun of somebody and that can hurt, if you laugh at the wrong time, but most laughter comes because of joy. That's why in Indian country they're always laughing. They should be crying, actually, but they're laughing. It's a form of protecting themselves.

JB: Is prayer needed by the natural world?

TP: I'm not sure what "prayer" means in English. If it's my definition of prayer, yes. And my definition is: When you take a moment to communicate with the spiritual life that surrounds you. If you do this enough, then you communicate with spiritual lives around you. They become important to you, and you find your place in peace and good mind. But if you don't, then you are imbalanced, unhappy, and ungrateful. You are just a greed-monster, like a bulldozer, without regard to life. Without prayer that's what you become; that's what society becomes, too, if it doesn't know how to pray.

Because, see, if the sun goes out, if the wind stops blowing, we all go out. If the Mother Earth stops growing the corn and the fruit, we're all going to go out. These are the things we need to ally with, the things we need to talk to and harmonize with. That harmony that we've had since the beginning of time is why we're here today.

Singing the World

An Interview with Heather Valencia

From PARABOLA Vol. 25, No. 2, "Riddle & Mystery"

Heather Valencia lived for many years on the Pascua Yaqui reservation just outside of Tucson, Arizona, with her husband, Anselmo Valencia, the spiritual leader of the Yaqui people. Of Cherokee and Welsh descent, Heather was a full participant in the spiritual and ritual traditions of the Yaqui people, and has taken on the responsibility of preserving and transmitting the Yaqui culture to younger generations. An accomplished artist, writer, and storyteller, she is the author of **Queen of Dreams: The Story of a Yaqui Dreaming Woman** (Fireside).

PARABOLA: What is your relationship to the Yaqui?

HEATHER VALENCIA: I am a dreaming woman born with memory of *sewa yo ania,* the enchanted flower world. Anselmo Valencia told me when we married that my spiritual work in this life was entwined with that of his people, and that I would serve as a Mother of the Deer Lodge, where the deer singers, the deer dancers, and all members of the Deer Lodge work together. For many years I had that honor and privilege. He told me further, that it would be my responsibility to help ensure that the memory of these teachings were kept alive for the children who come after us.

Ever since I was a child my soul has remembered this. The hummingbird is the Yaqui symbol for the sweet, sacred essence of joy that lives in the heart of the enchanted flower world. One of my first memories is of a hummingbird coming to me under a bower of jasmine when I was in a bassinet. Throughout my life the hummingbird has tracked me. When I was twenty-four years old, I was on a mountain called Oh Be Joyful in the high Rockies with my young son, and we ate the columbine flower for lunch one day. Shortly after that Anselmo and his best friend Kititu came to our cabin in the form of their *chilkin*. They tracked us through the hummingbird. I then began my journey to the southwest—to these people that were the most intrinsic part of my soul memory.

P: What is a chilkin?

HV: Chilkin is the Yaqui word for a dreaming double. If you have a dreaming double, you can be in two places at once. The dreaming double can go through light worlds and gather medicine and power. When Anselmo found me, I lived in the Rocky Mountains, which are a massive ore body. Wherever there is a high concentration of ore, if someone has the capacity to develop a dreaming double, it is enhanced there. That's why I'm sure I was led to the Rocky Mountains.

Arizona, where the Yaqui live, is a massive ore body, and it is the place where there are the most lightning strikes in the world. The earth actually calls the lightning down. The Yaqui word for lightning is *veveoktia,* and it is very important in their culture. They believe they have a special connection with the heart of the creator, and lightning is a vehicle to enhance that connection.

Right before I went to Arizona for the first time, I was in a tremendous lightning storm. After that, I was able to see the violet fire around myself and others. The Yaqui have a word for the violet fire that I cannot say: I have heard it said, but they speak the word only in ceremony because the violet fire is so sacred.

The violet fire is the key to the chilkin. When the violet fire is visible, it is the signal that the seer has returned to a place of perfected memory. When you look at a rainbow, you see that there are seven colors—from red to violet. The violet fire lives in the place between rainbows. It is an eternal place, and it is necessary to be alive in the completed world to reach this place.

P: So it's a mystery as well, at least from where we are. Can you tell us more about the deer singers and their role in the Deer Lodge?

HV: There are living worlds and worlds that, though once alive, have been eaten and no longer have life. It is the deer singer's role to keep alive that which is sacred and necessary in the enchanted flower world. He does that through the vibration of his songs. He does that by naming. The Yaqui believe that only through this method can the world be preserved. If the deer singer no longer names everything in the song, the living world will cease to exist. There is no song in the dead world.

The enchanted flower world is the five worlds combined in their original, subtle, shimmering perfection. It is a place of dreaming. From this place of dreaming human beings have named that which is, that which comes into being. Through the deer singer's song, life is maintained. Every single animal, every particle of dust, every rock, every rivulet, every plant, every cloud—all of these things are part of the deer singer's repertoire. There are many deer singers, and each one takes a lineage and a responsibility for keeping a part of the enchanted flower world alive.

P: Does each deer singer take responsibility for a particular realm—i.e., mineral, vegetable, etc?

HV: No, it's not like that. Anselmo was a very famous deer singer, and one of his most famous deer songs was about a bay horse. We are told that horses didn't exist in the New World until the Spaniards brought them, but the Yaqui don't remember it that way. They remember that there were horses here a long, long time ago, and then for a while the horses went away. And the bay horse actually is a tricolored horse with red, white, and black coloring—the three sacred colors of the Yaqui. The horse is a blood bay with a white star on its forehead. This was a very famous and ancient song from Anselmo's lineage. He also sang a certain little pig song from his lineage. He sang a very famous water song, a rock song, and a butterfly song. Sometimes he would sing other songs because he had seen a sick animal; he would sing a song for that animal to bring it back to its perfection.

The most beautiful expression I ever saw of that was when a little boy brought us a baby sparrow in the heat of *Sabado Gloria*. The baby sparrow was dying. The bird was given to me by Anselmo's son, and I showed it to Anselmo. He began the song of the sparrow, which he does not normally sing. But as he sang the tiny bird came back to life in my hand, and it trilled, an amazing, beautiful sound. It jumped up onto Anselmo's shoulder and trilled again, filling the deer lodge with song. And the third time the sparrow song was sung, it flew off into the morning, singing. That's how much power the deer songs have. They are sung according to the need of the moment, but people always request that certain songs be sung because they have a liking for them.

P: I remember you telling me that Anselmo, although he was well known for the many things he had achieved as a political leader of the Yaqui people—establishing them as a legal tribe in the U.S., getting them a homeland—as well as being a powerful medicine man and spiritual leader, the thing that he was most proud of and that was closest to his heart was his deer singing.

HV: Yes, and on the other side, in the enchanted flower world, that is what he always was and will be. That's the heart of his soul. He was the very finest deer singer. His songs were light and fast. The rhythm that he and his singers had was a quicker rhythm than anyone else's—very beautiful. He could sing for three days and three nights without sleeping because he was alive in the enchanted flower world when he was doing that work.

P: You mentioned that there were five worlds that combined into the enchanted flower world.

HV: According to my husband's people, the first world is the physical world. It is called the wilderness world, or *hu ania*. The second world is the mental world, called the enchanted world or *yo ania*. It is called enchanted because a mind is an individual thing. Even though all the human beings may be in one circle and experiencing one ceremony, each individual will have a different perception of it.

The third world is the shadow world, or night world, and this is called *tuka ania*. This is the crucible, the place where all the evolutionary work is done on the human being. This is the world that is the key to our soul memory.

The fourth world is the magical world and is called the sorcerer's world, or *sea ania*. The fifth world is a spiritual world—it is the dreaming place and is called *tenku ania*. Tenku is the word for the dream, the Great Dream.

In order not to be eaten or lost in the third world and to know how to navigate the place of the great mystery, one has to have training, knowledge, and ability. You need help from the beings in the fourth world to make it through the shadow. You can't get through by yourself.

The fifth world you cannot reach without heart, love, and willingness to sacrifice yourself for the tribe and Mother Earth. This world is only accessible through the heart. It is the most refined world, closest to the original dream, to the place of origin, which is the sun, the great central sun.

The Yaqui believe we have lots of lifetimes. We come from the sun to learn and to teach. We have to work to get back there. We try to return every time we die, but the corona of the sun burns us if we have anything left of the shadow or of shadow food in us, and the sun sends us back to try again. Only when you make your way all the way through to the fifth world can you return to the heart of the sun and not come back.

Anselmo said that when he died this time that was what he would do. He had done his work for his people many times, and he was tired and ready to go back to the sun. Everyone believes he did that. He died on May 2, called the Day of the Cross among the Yaqui. If you die on that day, it doesn't matter how much food for the shadow you have within you—the sun will burn it up like cottonwood in a sacred fire and let you go on through. In order to die on that day and get the benefit, you must state your intention beforehand, which is what Anselmo did. He said he would die on that day and he did. He was a fifth-world magician. Yaqui always know when they are going to die. They tell everybody goodbye two or three days before they are going and then they leave.

P: I have heard that the name Yaqui was given to them by outsiders and that it means "stubborn." What do the Yaqui call themselves?

HV: The Yaqui name for themselves is very beautiful. It is *Yoeme*. Yoeme means "the hidden ones, the hidden people."

P: What are they hidden from?

HV: They are hidden from denser worlds, the dead worlds. The dead cannot see the movement or penetrate the mystery of the Yoeme. The more alive something is, the more likely it is to see the Yoeme. The Yoeme are very pure, and in order to perceive them in their purest form you have to be at least a fourth-world magician. You know how if you're driving in a car and you say, "Do you see those rainbows and sundogs in the sky?" and someone else says, "No," you lend them your sunglasses and say, "Put these on, now do you see them?" Then they can see it, although they couldn't with their naked eye. The hidden ones are hidden in that way.

P: Do all these different worlds coexist in the same place?

HV: Yes, all these worlds exist within a human being, but the fourth and fifth worlds only exist in potential and have to be developed. There are many fifth-world dreamers among the Yaqui. The Yaqui came originally as fifth-world dreamers. This is a core teaching. The Yaqui believe first we dream and then the world becomes. They believe that it becomes through the vibration of song.

Knowledge is sought and mystery is revealed where that mystery originates, which is in the shadow. The shadow world is very cherished by the Yaqui, and Yaqui are darkside dreamwalkers because they have shadow mastery. They are very alive in the first two worlds, and the third world is teeming with life from all worlds that feed upon each other. In the third world, there are the hunter and the hunted. In this realm, to be alive and not be eaten one has to have a guide or a teacher to engage with the mystery and make a passage. But this is the fun of it all, this is the place where the Yaqui like to be. The Yaqui have power in the shadow world.

P: This is where the chilkin comes from?

HV: Yes.

P: Does everyone have a chilkin or the potential of one? Is it something that is developed or tamed?

HV: When the shadow double comes out like that, some kind of magic has occurred. One way to induce the chilkin to emerge is by eating sacred plants, whether by accident or on purpose. Although not all humans have the chilkin, all Yaqui do, because they drink the milk of their mother, and in their mother's milk is the essence of the sacred plants that cause one to have a dreaming double. This is something that is discussed with the children. Their parents will ask them, "Where did you go last night?" and they will reply, "I went to my aunt's house in Mexico last night and I saw that my cousin Antonia is sick." And then the aunt will call and confirm that she saw their child walking around and that Antonia is ill. The Yaqui get this from the very milk of their mother.

When a Yaqui baby is born, some dirt is put on the baby's tongue, and the baby remembers the shadow. The enchanted flower world is made from the sacrifice of the mother's blood. That is part of the teachings of the shadow world. In the shadow world there is the red, white, and black, but all together it looks black, so the shadow is hungry for red and white—it has to have it to keep existing. White comes from the fifth world and red comes from the first world.

Dreaming is very important to the Yaqui people. Teachings and communications are carried in dreams. Through the dreaming, it is known what's going on, what's coming up, what we need to work with at any given time.

Last month I was at a dreaming circle in Los Angeles, and a beautiful Yaqui woman named Francine, who was not raised in the Yaqui culture, told a dream where she was a mouse. There were many mouse relatives with her, and she recognized each and every one. They were all as individual as humans, all different. She knew that they were all political prisoners. The captors put them in a bathtub, and one mouse knew what do. He was wearing red, white, and black clothing, and he had the other mice form a triangle and thus escape from the bathtub.

As soon as Francine started telling the dream, I was reminded of the story of Baticumsekum (Yaqui for "where the water comes down") in the Sonora desert. During the Mexican-Yaqui war, all the Yaqui women, children, and elders at this place were locked into a church that was boarded up and then set afire by soldiers. The Yaqui turned into mice and escaped. The triangle is the secret battle formation of the Yaqui, given to Anabuluktec at the time of the Talking Tree.

I knew that Francine was truly Yaqui when she told me her dream and I knew she had had family at Baticumsekum. She was very happy to hear that and she's proud of her mouse medicine.

P: What is the story of the Talking Tree?

HV: A long time ago, after the time of the great lizards, the people were very, very happy. They only ate creatures of the sea and plants. Something very strange occurred one day. A great tree on Tosalkowee began to shake and vibrate, and the medicine people knew that the tree was talking. The talking of the tree greatly disturbed all the people, but no one could discern exactly what the tree was saying because they did not have any memory upon which to base the information. The wise people knew of a young girl who had come down recently from the stars. Her name was Itzcelli. She did not have a human father. They knew that this girl would understand the talk the tree was making. So the village elders made a journey up to the mountain where this girl lived with her mother. They told the mother that they needed Itzcelli's help, and the girl agreed to go with the village elders to listen to the tree. She sat for nine days beneath the tree, neither eating nor drinking, but receiving the information and crying. At the end of the nine days she came forward and told the elders what the tree had said. The enchanted flower-covered world in which the people were living so joyfully was about to come to an end because there were big people coming from a dense world across the sea. They were going to take the land of the people and kill them, they would want everything and there was no way they would be given enough—they would just want more. The leaders asked the girl what to do, and the girl said the tree had this message: "You can do one of three things. You can choose to stay here in the enchanted flower world, and you will remain as you are and can help the others in the other worlds. You can choose to go into the sea and become one with the enchanted people of the sea and offer help from there. Or you can choose to grow big and to go into the new world to stand up against these ones who are coming and to fight to keep them from taking your land. In order to do so, you will have to eat meat to grow big."

So the people were instructed by Itzcelli to ask Brother Deer, because he was the most beautiful and graceful of all the creatures, if he would make the sacrifice for them. He was the sweetest of all the meats. Brother Deer said he would be glad to make the sacrifice so that the people could grow big and keep their land. Because Brother Deer gave his life for the people, the Deer Dance began. The tree said, "You must say thank you to Brother Deer for allowing your world to continue, for giving you the bridge to the next world with his flesh." So they made the Deer Dance for him, and it is the most sacred and important of all dances to this day. The deer dancer is the most beloved of all the Yaqui people.

When someone dies, when he sheds his mortal flesh, there is a ceremony performed with the death dancers; they are the ones who wear the black, white, and red. They are the navigators of the shadow, and the navigators between worlds. They are called *pascola* dancers. A year later, the ones who died are considered to have been born again in new forms, and to celebrate their rebirth the deer dancers come. The deer dancer celebrates life, rebirth, and life in a new world. This was the gift and teaching of the talking tree.

When Itzcelli finished delivering her talk to the people, they had a final dance around the tree with all the people before they made their choices and separated. A beautiful violet flower bloomed on the tree from the breath of the deer, and at the end of the dance the red roses bloomed. The red rose is a sacred flower to the deer—it is what the deer like to eat best—and it is the flower worn on the horns of the deer dancer. Some of the people went to the sea, some became *surem,* the little enchanted people of the land and forest who watch over us, and the rest became the Yaqui of today.

Deer Song

Tosay Wikit
(WHITE BIRD)

In the spirit of Anselmo's teachings, I offer these Yaqui words, and only a loose translation:

The spider's web is transporting us, over there, to the forest of the flower-covered enchanted world.

> Tosalwikit tabnaka guitosalipo, yoleia
> Junamansu siali juya
> Biapa Culiachi guitsalita kalaguikti
> Jicaune bokapo jiak ne yoleilia hininan ne machika yolelia
> Tosalwikit tabnaka guitosalipo, yoleia

This is repeated three times. Three is the sacred number to the Yaqui, and songs are always performed in sets of three.

The "white bird" in this song is the gossamer web of Grandmother Spider moving gracefully on the breeze of the enchanted flower world. The images and feelings these songs convey are subtle and intricate—Anselmo told me there is no direct translation from Yaqui to any other language, and that we cannot dissect the Mystery, only surrender to it. In the presence of the music the being is taken to the sewa yo ania and is thrilled by the breath and heartbeat at the center of creation through the deer songs, which are the voice of the enchanted flower world.

Moving Through Milestones

An Interview with Sobonfu Somé

From PARABOLA Vol. 25, No. 4, "Fate and Fortune"

Sobonfu Somé, whose name means "keeper of the rituals, keeper of knowledge," is an initiated member of the Dagara tribe of Africa and the author of two books, **The Spirit of Intimacy** (Quill) and **Welcoming Spirit Home** (New World Library). She now lives in California, but spends time every year in the village where she was raised and where she has a large extended family.

PARABOLA: How is the idea of fate perceived in the Dagara culture? Is it completely predetermined, or is there free will?

SOBONFU SOMÉ: The whole concept of fate is taken very seriously in my culture; people pay a lot of attention to it. It's part of their daily life. When they wake up, what they are going to do is based on their fate and also on their life purpose.

Fate is something that is set in motion before we are born, through the decisions we make about coming here and what we want to do or give to this world, the kind of family we are born into, and where we arrive. Fate is also changeable in the African point of view; it depends on the kind of choices you make. Your fate can change depending on what you do with it.

P: Is it possible to avoid your fate? In many cultures there are stories about people who try very hard to avoid their fate only to find themselves fulfilling it despite their best efforts.

SS: Well, there's what we call changeable fate and fixed fate. The fate of every human being is eventually to die, and there's no getting around it. You can do all you want to try to prolong your life, but eventually you're still going to die.

There is also changeable fate. Depending on what you do, you can either change it or not change it. Our fate can be changed by the actions we take, by how tuned in we are to our inner voices and to the voices of others, and by what we do with our life. We can make our fate, we can push it further and further away, or we can make it happen quicker.

I'll tell you a story about a man whose fate it was to die by snakebite. One morning he went off into the woods to relieve himself, and he laid his clothes on the ground while he did so. Afterwards, when he went to get dressed, something told him to do a small divination. So he did, and said, "Hmm, it looks like something is going to kill me today."

He looked around him and didn't see any wild animals; he wasn't under a tree; there wasn't any lightning, and he wondered, "What could it be?" He saw nothing dangerous—but every time he went to pick up his outfit, something made him pause. Finally he found a stick and began to beat on his clothes, and when he shook them a snake slithered out—a small snake called the "five-minute snake" by my people because it is so poisonous that you would die within five minutes if you were bitten. If he had been bitten he would have died before he could have gotten back to the village for help.

It's about paying attention to signs and listening to that small inner voice. By being very diligent and acting on the warning he received from the divination, he was able to avert his fate. In the long run his fate might eventually catch up to him, but at least for the time being it didn't.

P: So listening and paying attention to signs is important?

SS: Yes. There are important milestones within our lives, placed there so that when we hit them we are reminded of our life purpose. The milestones that arise for us come in various forms: major illnesses, big changes, death, radical challenges that can destroy us if we are not strong enough to move through them.

Milestones were placed in our life by ourselves before we were born to serve as reminders, to shock us into remembering our life's purpose. Some of us can move through them by ourselves, and some of us need community to help us. Sometimes when we don't have enough support and we're not able to tune in, we end up hitting them and not being able to walk through them. We become unable to carry out our life purpose because we get stuck.

Paying attention to signs and tuning in is one way to work with our fate; doing ritual is another; having community and support around you is another plus. Being able to do divination to find out about the next fate coming into your life or what *the* fate is that you are to face this lifetime is helpful as well.

P: What forms of divination do the Dagara use?

SS: There are many forms of divination in my culture. Cowry shell divination is one; stones-and-bones divination is another; stick divination and water divination are others. One style can reveal more information in a particular area than another. If I don't want to hear all the things I might have to do I can pick a system of divination that will not give me as severe an outlook or prescription.

P: Do you recommend doing your own divination or having someone else do it for you?

SS: It depends on your level of honesty. *(laughs)* You can do a wonderful divination for yourself. I know at times when I have done a divination for myself, the temptation to interpret the signs in the way I want to see them is very great, because I don't want to hear anything negative. I may see that the signs show that I'm going to have an accident, but I'll decide that it just means I'm going to have some difficulty, and not worry about it. As a result I don't pay attention, and of course things still happen. One of the worst ways to negatively influence your own fate is to do your own divination and then refuse to look at the signs as they are. We're too busy trying to make ourselves feel comfortable in the moment and often we don't pay attention to what is actually happening.

Being able to do a divination for yourself really requires a high level of honesty. It's often best to have other people do the divination for you because they are more likely to tell you the truth no matter what it might sound like. However, sometimes the elders in my village hesitate to tell people who come for a divination what fate they have if they can't see that they are going to have the will to change it. When you talk about fate with people who don't have a supportive community, it may bring on their fate faster because they don't have a grounding force around them. They may end up worrying about it to the point of not being able to pass beyond it or take any steps to change it. By *not* hearing about it, they can actually live longer and might inadvertently be able to change their fate. Not telling them might actually create more possibility for change.

P: Community is important because we are able to guide each other through milestones and provide information and support?

SS: The way a community can help you is by noticing where you are heading. If you cannot move, if you are frozen in a milestone, they can take steps to help you move out of that state and through the milestone. We help each other to hold our fate.

Milestones are often a reminder that we are going in the right direction, even though it might not feel like it while it's happening—it may feel completely chaotic, completely distressing. But out of chaos come order and life. Out of chaos come the most marvelous gifts. That's why we have a saying that where the wound is, the gift also is. Out of the wound is born the gift.

P: In your book you talk about the hearing ritual that is done when a woman is pregnant. Could you speak more about that?

SS: The hearing ritual is one of many Dagara rituals performed throughout the process of pregnancy and childbirth. Its purpose is to hear from the unborn child what that child is coming here to do, what its purpose is, and what it needs to support it in that purpose—what kind of food is good for its spirit, what colors are good for its spirit, and what it might need to be surrounded with so that its fate doesn't end up taking it away sooner rather than later.

All along we have been listening to the soul of the unborn child and paying attention to what it is saying. That's why, for instance, when a pregnant woman in my village cries, people don't look at her and say, "Oh, she's just getting emotional again." Instead she is seen as giving voice to what the unborn child is feeling.

After the hearing ritual, a name is chosen to match the child's purpose in life. The name should be strong enough to defeat fate and help the child overcome all the milestones in its life. When deciding to give a name to a child, it is very important to listen to what the child is saying. To have a name put on you is a huge responsibility. If the name's not appropriate, your spirit can crumble under its weight.

It doesn't matter which tradition we come from. The meaning of our name influences us positively or negatively and can actually quicken our fate and determine the kind of life we end up living—whether we are frozen in our fate or able to move forward. I am trying to do a small study here on the different meanings of names. I have followed several people with the same name, and they have certain patterns in their lives that are very similar. It's not just a cultural thing; it's a universal phenomenon. Language is very powerful—thoughts, words are all very powerful and can create "weather" around us.

P: In some spiritual traditions you are given a new name at a certain point, perhaps recognizing that by making this change in your life you are changing your fate, putting yourself under new influences. Do you believe that changing your name changes your fate and fortune as well?

SS: Yes, and more. Changing your name definitely changes your fate. No doubt about that. However, I don't want people to be under the impression that if your fate is going downhill that you should change your name and that will fix it. When you change your name, at least in my tradition, the name will not immediately come alive. It takes about five years for a name to kick in. That's why they say by the time you are five years old, your name has grown onto you. You have become your name.

We should be careful about what name we choose. It's very important to meditate on the name and feel the kind of responsibility we would be taking on with it and to see how we would be able to live with that, because once you've taken it on, it's on, and that's going to be your fate. And of course we all want a *grand* fate, something positive, something wonderful—we'll do anything to have that, but in our excitement we can make a poor choice.

There's a need to say goodbye to the old name you had. Otherwise its fate may linger behind like a ghost and haunt you even though you have embarked on a new fate. And there's a need to take the new name on ceremonially, as it was done when you were born.

P: You said earlier that ritual was another important way to move through milestones or to work with your fate. How does that work?

SS: Ritual is a way of continuous prayer and feeding the soul. Just like our body needs food and drink to survive, so our soul needs ritual for food. Certain rituals can change my fate positively—by doing something as small as giving an egg to the nature spirit. Ritual helps create a pathway through whatever milestone is before you. One beneficial ritual that can be done yearly is to give something away on behalf of your spirit—something dear to you. Or you might prepare a feast for others. Something as simple as providing a feast once a year can change a certain aspect of your fate in a very positive way.

It's very important to notice that seemingly negative life events are sometimes positive. For example, a life-threatening illness that takes you to the other side—that is a major milestone you went through that completely changed your life. It is when you go through something like that and *nothing* changes that you should worry.

P: Do the Dagara believe that dreams are a way of accessing or affecting our fate?

SS: Dreams are definitely a way of accessing our fate. Dreams are a way for the soul to come alive and to point out those things that we are not willing to look at in our life. Powerful dreamers can see the fate of other people and tell them where they are heading.

I remember when I was a child, when somebody was going to die, I would dream it in vivid detail, and I often knew, depending on the symbol, that it was an unchangeable fate—there was nothing I or anyone else could do to change it. Every single time I would have those dreams where a loved one died I got so heartbroken. I had to demand that the way the dreams came be less frightening for me, because at the time I would see *exactly* how someone was going to die. It's still the same, really; I still dream the signs, but at least I don't have to go through the pain of seeing them draw their last breath. It was too big a responsibility for me to keep.

What I see happening in dreams tells me my fate, the fate of the people around me, and the fate of the universe. Dreams are very important. Some people believe they are meaningless, that because we were thinking about somebody we have a dream about them. But even to think of someone means we have tapped into their spirit. Dreams take us closer to them and reveal what is going on within their souls. We believe if you dream about someone it's important to tell them what you saw in your dream.

P: Is there also a greater community fate or universal fate?

SS: There are all of those in the universe. Our personal fate has the capacity to influence our community and also the universe. Not paying attention to one's personal fate can influence the whole world. By making a positive change in our fate we make a positive change in the whole world, the whole universe. Even those who are stuck, who are frozen in their fate, are then able to move forward because of the positive influence of others.

P: Then what we do personally has an influence much greater than on the personal level?

SS: Yes, the root goes deep and the branches touch the whole universe. What we do with our fate is important, not just for our own sake, but for the sake of the universe.

Approaching Presence

The Silent
Guide

FATHER BEDE GRIFFITHS

Vol. 11, No. 1
"The Witness"

Awakening
to the Present

**FATHER THOMAS
KEATING**

Vol. 15, No. 1
"Time & Presence"

Inviting Hell
into Heaven

WILLIAM SEGAL

Vol. 24, No. 2
"Prayer & Meditation"

Reaching for the Trapeze

PETER BROOK

Vol. 15, No. 1
"Time & Presence"

The Command Is to Hear

RABBI ADIN STEINSALTZ

Vol. 19, No. 1
"The Call"

The Experience of Change

**TENZIN GYATSO
(H.H. THE DALAI LAMA)**

Vol. 15, No. 1
"Time & Presence"

The Silent Guide

An Interview with Father Bede Griffiths

From PARABOLA Vol. 11, No. 1, "The Witness"

After becoming a Benedictine monk, **Father Bede Griffiths** traveled to India where he presided over Saccidananda Ashram, a house of prayer and retreat in the rural countryside west of Tiruchirapalli on the shores of the sacred river Cavery. Father Griffiths's books include the contemporary spiritual classics **The Golden String, The Return to the Center,** and **The Marriage of the East and the West** (Templegate Publishers).

PARABOLA: Do you have a definition of what a witness means in the context of religion?

FATHER BEDE GRIFFITHS: In meditation one tries to calm the body and the senses, to calm the mind, and become what's called "the silent witness," the witness beyond the mind. We in the West think that the mind is everything, but all Eastern practice is to get beyond the mind to the point of the silent witness, where you're witnessing yourself, where you've gone beyond the ego, beyond the self.

The Indian tradition rests on what the West has largely lost: that there are three levels. There is the level of the body and the level of the mind, which the Western world thinks is the end. But beyond the body is the spirit. It's the *Atman,* the *pneuma* of St. Paul, another dimension where we go beyond the mind, the senses, and the feelings, and we're aware of the transcendent reality. And that is the goal of life, to get to that.

P: How do you see the development of the capacity to witness validly? What is involved in that?

BG: The supreme example of this in Hinduism is the guru who is regarded as able to fully awaken a person. But I think that at almost any level there can be a sharing—you see, we do actually influence the mind of the person we're talking to, and someone who has gone beyond the mind can help others to go beyond it.

P: The West, it seems to me, resists the concept of the guru, someone one has to obey.

BG: I do think it's true that the guru has a deeper insight and that he can awaken it in others, but the idea that one simply surrenders to the guru I find rather dangerous. It can help people at a certain stage, without a doubt, but equally it can lead to a sort of infantilism where you may lose your ego but you also lose your own dynamism and your own identity. The Indian temperament tends toward total surrender to the guru, but frequently there is little growth. And it can be very bad for the guru; he can become inflated if he's not careful, you see.

P: The final guru is the witness inside us.

BG: Yes, but it's very tricky. You can reach quite a deep level of experience, but the ego is always there behind. It can always come up again, and sometimes you don't recognize it. There are some gurus who are really very egoistic. I remember one very well-known guru whom I respect saying of another one that he was ego from head to foot.

P: What about the dependence, or independence, of witnessing on faith?

BG: I see faith as awakening to the transcendent. In the Christian perspective we say God is beyond the reason, beyond the created world altogether, and it's necessary to open the heart and the mind to the transcendent. Normally the transcendent manifests through some particular tradition. This seems to be where the religions differ. If you awaken to it in the Buddhist tradition you name it Nirvana and you enter into the Eight-Fold Noble Path and so on. And if you're a Hindu you name it Brahman or Atman and take the path of yoga, and if you're a Christian you name it God the Father and you enter into the path of Christ. So each is a path to the Supreme, having its own unique character.

P: What do you see as the purpose and the function of monastic life in regard to witnessing?

BG: This awakening can take place under any circumstances, and does so. But if it's to be nourished and to grow, most people need a time apart. And many need not only a time, but a life. A monastery or an ashram is a place which exists precisely to enable people both to awaken and to grow in their awareness of the transcendent.

P: At a very sensitive period in their development.

BG: Yes. And it can be temporary. In Buddhism particularly there is temporary monasticism, and many of us feel we should have temporary Christian monasticism. But in our tradition, normally, it's for life. You need centers where people can find this experience, and in the center you need one or two people, at least, who are fully committed to it. The Benedictine monk is one who is committed to this search, the experience of God, and who creates a center where others can find it.

P: It isn't so easy to establish such a center, obviously, from your own experience.

BG: And today perhaps more difficult than ever, because the rational mind is taking over everywhere. Science and technology make such incredible advances and people become more and more absorbed in them. That's entirely on the level of the rational mind, and people begin to think there's nothing beyond it. So it becomes more difficult now. And many people think that those who withdraw from the activity of life are not quite balanced or are escapists. But two things are happening. One is that the old system of science and technology is going on with marvelous developments, but the other is that there's been a breakthrough in science, in physics particularly, and an opening onto deeper levels of consciousness.

P: This has been going on for some time.

BG: This has been going on for some time, and I feel that this movement is the hope for the future. In that sense it's becoming easier, but the main movement is still towards the advance of technology.

P: Do you think there is an exoteric and an esoteric tradition in witnessing?

BG: I don't normally make that distinction as much as some people do. Especially in Christianity, I'm more inclined to think that the esoteric exists within the exoteric. They're not two separate movements. Many people see only the more outer surface of religion, but there are always some who can see the inner depth of it. I think that Augustine or St. Thomas Aquinas were right at the center of the esoteric church, while remaining with the exoteric.

P: So there's always an access. . . .

BG: Yes. I'm a Christian because I do believe that within the Christian churches, however external they are, the Holy Spirit is always present.

P: What about the relationship between morality and the witness?

BG: This is rather difficult. Quite a high level of spiritual experience can still leave people without much moral development. Actually, I make a distinction here between the psychic and the spiritual. When you get into the world of meditation, you enter into the psychic world that is beyond the physical. All of parapsychology is there—clairvoyance, healing powers, and so on—and that world is both good and evil. You can go through it to the spiritual which transcends the psychic, and which properly is the world and realm of the witness. But the whole of the vast psychic world is in between, as it were, and people can get caught in it. And it can be positively evil. I think a man like Rajneesh has tremendous psychic power—but he's not a spiritual man at all. So it's totally ambivalent—it can be good and evil. And it's very difficult to separate them.

P: What of the witness in relation to compassion?

BG: That is very fundamental, I think. As you go beyond the mind with all its divisions into good and evil, and right and wrong, you come to infinite compassion. You've gone beyond all the limits and now you can see everything in a much deeper perspective. I think it's almost the sign of a genuine spiritual experience. Take Buddhism—it's very remarkable. You have a vast method of meditation and discipline, and at the heart of it there's this extraordinary compassion. Normally, you can tell a genuine master—a Zen master or a Hindu yogi—precisely by that; when you see their compassion, you know that they are genuine. When you don't see the compassion, they are highly suspect.

Although there are differences. Buddhist compassion is not quite the same as the Hindu devotion and love, and that's still not quite the same as the Christian *agape*. Each has its own distinctive character.

P: What do you see in regard to bearing witness to what you have witnessed inside yourself?

BG: In India, we're very much concerned with the whole problem of poverty and suffering, and the feeling is very strong—particularly among Christians but also among Hindus—that a genuinely spiritual person must have concern for the poor and the suffering. So it links up with the problem of compassion. As you go deeper into your inner self and discover the transcendent mystery within, you become more open to the sufferings of people, to the problems of the world. We've had a tradition in the Catholic Church of separating active and contemplative lives. Some people are active and go into the world; some are contemplative and they leave the world and meditate. I think that's an artificial division. What is really wanted is very difficult. There are two different movements: one is withdrawal from the world in total silence and solitude; and the other is at the same time to have an openness horizontally. So there is a vertical and a horizontal movement which has a dual rhythm, a polarity which you have to discover.

P: Who are the ones in the Christian tradition who would exemplify this?

BG: It's fairly common in the Christian tradition, really; Jesus Himself is the best witness of all. We sometimes forget that while He went about doing good, He was also at the same time in communion with the Father. Jesus was living in that communion with the Father, that inner Witness, and from that all His work, all His teaching, followed. It's typical of the Christian tradition, but unfortunately in the last two or three centuries we've rather gone over to the active side, and there are not many witnesses to a really profound contemplative experience.

P: When do you feel that one is ready to witness in the world?

BG: Normally, I think, the witness itself tells you. This is very important. As you become more and more aware of the guide within, your outer life is guided as to when and where to act. It's delicate, because some people get worried that they ought to be doing more, but I think you have to wait until the guidance comes.

P: Where does martyrdom and asceticism enter into this process?

BG: I think that martyrdom is simply when your inner experience brings you into conflict with forces without, and the guide tells you that this is fundamental, you must give your life for this.

Asceticism is a difficult subject. It can be an obstacle. The ego can get into asceticism very easily, in the mastering of the body and the mind and the senses. So I always feel that while asceticism has a certain value, it must always proceed in relation to the inner experience. And asceticism should come from within. It should be an inner guide which tells you, "Do this," or "Don't do that," rather than something you impose on yourself.

P: I'm interested in the whole idea of witnessing to another religious tradition—the crossover, in which you are involved.

BG: That is extremely important. There I find two dangers. The danger in the West until recently has been to see all religions as completely separate, and even opposed. But the danger in the East is the opposite, and that is to say that all religions are the same, that there is no real difference at all. We have to learn to see the unity and distinction. Each religion has its unique character. We must respect that. For the Christians, it's very important. There is a unique Christian gospel and message that we want to share with others. But at the same time we need to recognize that there is a unique message in Hinduism and in Buddhism, which we need to share as well.

When I first came to India, I attended a very interesting meeting in Bangalore of the Union for the Study of the Great Religions. It was founded by Radakrishnan, when he was a professor at Oxford. Radakrishnan actually came to the meeting. We had representatives of all the religions of India there, witnessing to their own religion. It was held at Theosophical Hall, and there were quite a number of Theosophists there, and they were all saying, "We must get beyond all these religions and meet in pure spiritual truth." That is the opposite, you see. I think you must live within your tradition, respect the others, and grow towards unity. But don't mix them all up or think there's another way you can get beyond them all.

P: When would you say that you began your own witnessing?

BG: Inner or outer? Well, I had very deep experiences which I recorded in *The Golden String* and that set me on the path. And then I was twenty years in the monastery in England and I was witnessing in a way. I wrote a good deal, in a small way. I always felt that I was living for others; I never felt that I was living just for myself. But I suppose the critical time came when I felt the attraction for India and was given the opportunity to come. And then it was a quite definite effort to try to witness to the Christian tradition of contemplation within the context of the Hindu and Buddhist.

P: How do you feel that your witnessing to the Indian people has proceeded? Are they opening out to it?

BG: Yes and no. If you try to witness to a contemplative tradition, to the spiritually transcendent in Christianity, Hindus are deeply interested and impressed. But they don't see the differences in it. They see you as a holy man, even a saint, but they don't see the difference, you see. So I think the task is to witness to a distinctive Christian contemplative life—which is at the same time open to the Hindu, to the Buddhist, and to other religions.

P: How would you distinguish between the missionary thrust and the genuine witnessing?

BG: I don't see any point in a kind of evangelical witness which is not a witness to the spirit. As Mahatma Gandhi used to say, "You should spread the Gospel as a rose would spread its scent." Something that comes from your heart and from your life and from your whole inner being—and then that is convincing.

P: I wonder about witnessing in relation to self-realization or ecstasy.

BG: The silent witness: that really is self-realization. It's finding the real self, which is the witness behind the active self. I always understand it in the Christian sense of the spirit, the pneuma of St. Paul; and that is the capacity for God in each human person. There's this point of the spirit beyond the body, beyond the soul with all of its activities; there's a point of the spirit where we're open to God. It's the point of our openness to the Divine. And that is the point of witness and of self-realization. The spirit is the principle of the self: the Divine self manifesting in that human self at the point of the spirit.

P: And this would be synonymous with ecstasy?

BG: Well, now, ecstasy has two senses, you see. One is when you lose consciousness of the body-soul, and you're only experiencing the spirit. I think much more normal is an awakening to the spirit, to the presence of God within, while remaining fully conscious of the physical, the psychosomatic level.

Normally when people speak of ecstasy they mean a going out of your present consciousness into a state of trance or something like that. To me it's important that the experience of God, of the true self, does not destroy or in any way inhibit the lower self, the psychophysical organism, which is your means of experience and of expression. You go beyond it, but you don't reject or deny it.

P: What about the body? What is its function in the witness?

BG: I was particularly interested in that number of PARABOLA on "The Body." I feel that in the Christian view, which I share, the body is of very great importance. There is a tendency in certain forms of Hinduism, certainly, to think that the purpose of spiritual exercises is to get beyond the body. But in my understanding, the human being is body-soul-spirit, and it's an integrated whole. Body and soul—the body is dependent upon and integrated with soul, and body and soul are dependent upon and integrated in spirit. The body is part of the wholeness of the human being. And that's why incarnation is very important. God enters into the psychophysical realm and assumes it and doesn't discard it. And at the resurrection the body is not discarded, it is assumed into the life with the soul and the spirit.

P: You would be suspicious of ascetic practices.

BG: Yes, I'm very suspicious. I think the place of the body is a significant part of the Christian contribution. I always like to quote St. Paul: "Your body is the temple of the Holy Spirit." Glorify God in your body. And another very interesting one, "The body is not for fornication but for the Lord." The same body which fornicates is for the Lord. So it's the total human being which is to enter into the life of the spirit.

P: There is a long tradition of the punishing of the body in all religions.

BG: I think it's particularly bad in Christianity. Punishing the body and suppressing the senses, the feelings, and the imagination—it's a method, and it can work for those who have strong will and character. They can attain to the spirit through that sort of negative approach. But for many people it's disastrous. They precisely need to strengthen the body and the senses and the feelings. Many people begin on a path from the emotions, and if you emphasize the soul and the mind and the will you're stressing the very thing that needs to be calmed down.

P: What was Christ's concept of witnessing? I've always been confused by the idea that you should not hide your light under a bushel, yet you must withdraw to pray. Those two concepts always seemed to me to be contradictory.

BG: Jesus Himself is witnessing, not so much in what He says or what He does, but He Himself is bearing witness to the Father. So the two sides are there. For a Hindu, you go to the holy man, simply to see him, feel the presence, and not so much to hear any words. The holy man witnesses by his silence. You have to be open to it and to come into the presence. The Christian is sent out, to preach and to teach. The two are present in both, however. The life of the Buddha is a supreme example. I think we have to realize—and Western people find this difficult—that any kind of external word, preaching, or teaching, is secondary to the inner reality, the inner self, the inner experience. That is what we have to learn. So many Christians think the whole thing is going out preaching and teaching.

P: If you have this gift for evangelism, it's very tempting to use it.

BG: And it's very difficult for your ego not to get into it.

P: What about the danger in connection with premature witnessing?

BG: It's very serious. Your own ego gets into it, you forget that it's the Divine Himself who has come through your ego, and you confuse the Divine with the ego. That's disastrous.

Many Christian saints, monks in particular, fled from people when they had a conversion experience. People would flock to them and they would flee further away, to the desert. They were so afraid of getting involved in the ego in that way. They had an experience of the spirit, and people coming to see them and agitating them in so many ways prevented that inner growth, that inner experience, which to them was the reality.

P: Would there be a point when they would feel certain enough and strong enough so they could go back?

BG: They varied, you know. St. Anthony's the best example. He spent twenty years in the desert, fled from everybody, but then people came to him and he came out and preached in the most marvelous way. But there were others who would feel this pressure around them which would lead them to seek greater solitude.

P: There is a danger, it would seem to me, of premature witnessing, in one who has had a conversion experience and who immediately wants to go out and convert the world.

BG: Exactly, yes. You confuse your own particular experience with the universal element in it. Every conversion is a discovery of the absolute in some measure, within a particular, limited human context. And you think your own context is the only truth. You experience the absolute in a unique way, and later confuse the absolute with the unique way in which you've experienced it.

Awakening to the Present

An Interview with Father Thomas Keating

From PARABOLA Vol. 15, No. 1, "Time & Presence"

Father Thomas Keating is a monk of the Cistercian order at St. Benedict's Monastery in Snowmass, Colorado. He is best known as an advocate of centering prayer, a personal practice of contemplative silence through the use of a sacred word or a sacred image. He is also the author of several books, including **The Mystery of Christ** and **Open Mind, Open Heart** (Amity House). In the mid-1980s he founded Contemplative Outreach, a program to offer information about the contemplative life to all Christians.

Cynthia Bourgeault teaches writing at the University of Maine at Augusta and is an ordained Episcopalian priest.

CYNTHIA BOURGEAULT: You've talked in your book *The Mystery of Christ* about living in two kinds of time, ordinary time and eternal time. Can you tell us what you mean by these two times?

FATHER THOMAS KEATING: Eternal time implies the values of eternity, which transcend ordinary time, breaking into linear time. Besides the three-dimensional world of time and space, there is the *source* of it that is always present, too, as the chief aspect of every reality. And its values are totally encompassing and embrace all time as if in an eternal embrace. So all of eternity is present in each moment of time for the person or seeker who has interiorized those values.

CB: The moment itself takes place in chronological time?

TK: Yes, chronological time keeps moving. Now in this context you could also conceive of it as circular time. Chronological time is a favorite view of the Western world; circular time, which is perhaps closer to the natural cycles, is more in honor in the Eastern religions. But in either case—whether you conceive of it as circular or linear, going toward an end point—eternal time, since it transcends the space/time continuum, is present in every moment. And this is what makes every moment of ordinary time extraordinary.

CB: We don't seem to *feel* it as extraordinary very often.

TK: That's because our perception of it is ordinary, meaning nothing is happening. But in actual fact, everything is happening in every moment—

CB: —if we could only wake up to it?

TK: That's what awakening really is. It's awakening to the full value of each moment of time, as penetrated by eternal values. And along with eternity, of course, go all the intuitive and unitive values of oneness that are covered over by the perception of categories and divisions on the mental-egoic, or rational, levels—especially in cultures cut off from their contemplative traditions and roots. At a deeper or higher, or what I prefer to call a more *centered* level, a movement toward our own center is really a movement toward everybody's center, which is the oneness of the ultimate unifying source of all creation. In other words, individuals are bound together by a unifying force which is present but not normally perceived, given the human condition, without the discipline of a practice that penetrates the mystery of ordinary time.

CB: Are you speaking only of our present Western culture here, or of the human predicament?

TK: The human predicament. All world religions seem to agree that our present state of evolutionary consciousness is a mess. We suffer from illusion—not knowing what true happiness is—and from concupiscence, which is a desire for the wrong things, or too much of the good things. And then if we ever discover the path to true happiness, our will or energy is too weak to pursue it anyway. This is classically what Christians mean by "the consequences of original sin," but in Hinduism you have *maya*—the same basic understanding that something is radically missing or wrong with the present state of consciousness that everybody, the human family, seems to have. Some religions depict this by the story of a fall from some happier or grace-filled state. So in the desperate need to find happiness which seems to be deeply rooted in every human being, we begin to develop emotional programs to shore up the fragile ego, to compensate for the happiness we can no longer find in the intimate experience of the source of our life. When a sense of connection to that source has been lost, almost anything seems better than to endure the emptiness, boredom, alienation—perhaps existential dread—that goes with feeling one's sense of isolation in a potentially hostile universe.

CB: Isn't there some part of us which actively resists this reconnecting? Is there something in us that clings to our usual sense of time? Do we have to fight our way down to the unitive source?

TK: I would think that it's usually experienced that way. That's why you get images in the different traditions of the warrior, or the spiritual combat—because it *is* a war. The false sense does not just drop dead on request; it's very firmly grounded in the subconscious—so much so that even when we buy into the spiritual journey and its values consciously, the false self just laughs at them and keeps right on going. And hence one experiences this battle between what one wants to do and what one actually does, still under the influence of the unconscious. So the heart of the *ascesis*, really, is in trying to dismantle the unconscious values, and these do not change unless you go after them deliberately. That's why you can have people in religious circles or on the spiritual journey who have given up all kinds of things and have changed to a new lifestyle, but unless you ask the false self to change, nothing really changes. It's the same worldliness under perhaps a more respectable façade.

CB: So what's needed is a change in attitude.

TK: Yes, and this is hard to come by, because the false self is so firmly in place when we begin to be self-conscious. And so its influence in our lives is extremely powerful and subtle unless we directly confront it and try to dismantle it—unless, as the Buddhists say, we "try to develop a mind that clings to nothing."

CB: Earlier you spoke of the need for "the discipline of a practice that penetrates the mystery of ordinary time." Were you thinking specifically of centering prayer here?

TK: Centering prayer is a method to introduce the dynamic of contemplation in the Christian tradition. By bracketing, so to speak, the ordinary flow of thoughts for a designated period of time in order to seek God at the intuitive level, it gives the practitioner a rest from the usual flow of thoughts which tend to reinforce or strengthen the objects of desire of the false self system. So it's a way of beginning to wake up to the eternal values that were always there but just drowned out by this racket of restless desires and desperate needs.

CB: I wonder if this doesn't exist in almost every tradition, this stilling and stopping in the present moment.

TK: It's essential in every tradition in some form, and there are a variety of forms to reach it. By the very act of letting go of the usual flow of thoughts during a regularly repeated time of prayer, one is experiencing some silence, some solitude, a certain simplicity in one's life, and a discipline of prayer. In every tradition these are the four ingredients of a contemplative lifestyle, and in actual fact they have a certain spontaneous capacity to express themselves in a change in daily life by accessing a level of rest, of well-being, that is deeper than ordinary sleep. But in the Christian tradition one has a personal relationship with Christ or with God. One is praying not just for an experience of rest, but to deepen one's relationship with God, which in turn prepares one to be able to face the dark side of the unconscious. Unless we are inwardly translating that experience of rest into practice and an inner freedom, then the experience is simply a high-class tranquilizer.

CB: Does this, in turn, have anything to do with Saint Paul's injunction to "pray without ceasing"?

TK: The real meaning of praying without ceasing, it seems to me, is that the divine presence or eternal values in the present moment begin to become more transparent; they become a kind of fourth dimension of the three-dimensional world. The awareness of God's presence at the subtlest level of all realities begins to be a kind of spontaneous addition to ordinary awareness, not through a thought or through any effort of ours at the time, but simply because it's there, and our capacity to perceive it has awakened through progress in contemplative prayer. Accessing the divine presence within ourselves seems to unlock the capacity to perceive it in all events, however opaque they may seem to the ordinary human perceptions. So to pray without ceasing is to be aware of the divine presence all the time as a spontaneous part of all reality.

CB: So far we've spoken of contemplative prayer as an individual's personal relationship to God. Isn't there a similarity in the way that a religious community as a group can make that relationship through liturgy, particularly the Eucharist?

TK: Oh, absolutely. Perhaps for most of us it is regular participation in worship that puts us in touch with eternal values on a regular, recurring basis. In the Old Testament the Sabbath seems to have had this purpose in view, and the Sunday for Christians is simply another way of celebrating a kind of peak moment in ordinary time in which the access to eternal time is particularly strong, usually because of the congregation of worshipping individuals who are trying to be in touch with divine energy.

CB: Is liturgy for the community, or is it also for the individual? And what does it give the individual that contemplative prayer couldn't?

TK: Fortunately, they have a friendly relationship, so that any growth in one is a growth in the other and they tend to reinforce each other; in other words, the best preparation for Eucharist is a deepening contemplative attitude. And actually contemplation is itself a social event because it's a real participation in the interior passion and death of Christ, which is the paradigm of what's going on within us. In other words, we, too, are experiencing the death of the false self, which Christians believe is what's meant by Christ taking on the human condition, becoming flesh. Flesh means the human condition in its fallen state, and this is what we believe the Son of God has taken on himself.

CB: Can you say a little more about the liturgical year—how that deepens and expands the various moments of the liturgy on a regular, cyclic basis?

TK: Each moment of time, obviously, is fairly brief, at least from our perspective. So even though the whole of the mystery of Christ is contained in one Eucharist, it helps if you can "open the package" somewhat and separate the parts so as to concentrate on one aspect of this living and dynamic mystery which can be totally communicated in one moment but, given the human faculties, can be much better assimilated by a gradual initiation into each mystery as it appears in a cycle. Depending on where you are in your own process, you also are going to perceive in the liturgy and identify with one process more than another because that's the one that's going on in you at this time. When that mystery recycles, it deepens awareness. Eventually you have integrated or assimilated them all, and then you *become* the word of God; in other words, you've heard it now at ever-deepening levels. Ultimately, the gospel is addressed to our inmost being and really hasn't been heard until that final level has been engaged. And then all the other levels become awakened and enriched because once it has reached the center and penetrated the mystery, all the symbols become more transparent and all other forms of prayer are enriched without one depending on them as a substitute for the mystery itself.

There's a marvelous wisdom in the liturgical year which teaches the whole of spiritual theology in a practical, dramatized way. Only unlike any other kind of drama, you're not just watching it—you are in the drama and the drama is in you. Thus in the drama of the death and resurrection of Christ, first comes the purification that Lent represents: a confrontation with the false self in order to dismantle it, with the help of grace.

After Lent, one has been purified to enter into the Easter and Pentecost mysteries, which are resurrection experiences of the fruit of having been freed from some degree of our false self through the Lenten practice. And year by year as this goes on, one is celebrating in the liturgy one's interior experience both of purification and resurrection.

Pentecost celebrates the completion of the cycle. Pentecost is the fullness of the Holy Spirit, the full illumination of the Pentecostal grace, which is to see reality from the perspective of divine wisdom, which is love. And remember that the liturgical year reads the gospel in the light of Pentecost, not in the light of the synoptic Gospels themselves.

CB: But doesn't the liturgical calendar use the phrase "ordinary time" for the period between Pentecost and Advent?

TK: Yes, that's what it's called. But all time is extraordinary when seen from the perspective of the Spirit.

CB: But just as we lose or ignore the importance of ordinary time in our everyday life, it seems that we also downplay the importance of ordinary time in the liturgical year. We wait around for the big feast days of Christmas, Easter, and Pentecost, and the rest of the year we feel we don't have to go to mass; it's not a "peak experience."

TK: But the whole purpose of the big feasts is to awaken us to the importance of ordinary time. And you see that in contemplatives. After a while they prefer the ferial days of ordinary time because these days don't have the sharp focus of a particular feast, but rather communicate the simple fact of the whole of the reality given you in the humble symbols of bread and wine, of eating and drinking.

In other words, all of life is to be transformed. The Eucharist really means that the whole universe is the body of God, so whatever its manifestation, you're always touching, seeing, sensing, feeling God. And the consciousness that is spontaneously aware of this deepest level of reality is totally present to these simple things because now everything is a total reve-lation of God, whether you're in church or outside of church. So the real reason to go to church is to be able to get along without it; that is to say, you have become the temple of God. Corporate worship is then a cel-ebration of the ongoing experience.

Inviting Hell into Heaven

An Interview with William Segal

From PARABOLA Vol. 24, No. 2, "Prayer & Meditation"

William Segal, painter and writer, began his career as a journalist. He met P. D. Ouspensky and G. I. Gurdjieff in the 1940s, and later spent long periods at the main Rinzai and Soto Zen monasteries in Japan. He is the author of a number of philosophical essays.

PARABOLA: What is your definition of prayer?

WILLIAM SEGAL: I think we can accept that prayer is the expression of a human need. People want something, and prayer enables them to express their desire. Prayer may be at different levels, from supplication, wishing for something tangible, to a wishing for something that is neither tangible nor material.

P: That was my next question: What are the levels of prayer? Obviously there are very primitive forms of prayer, and prayer that can be humanity's ultimate activity.

WS: Exactly. There is prayer which has to do with the simple needs of body and mind. And then there is prayer which has nothing to do with wanting something, where the impulse is for the highest.

Perhaps it is still asking for something, but what the highest prayer is asking for is unity with the supreme being, communion. Questions of levels can be very important because most prayers are directed toward the material level, but the highest are toward the ultimate psychic energy.

P: Can we actually change ourselves through prayer and achieve a higher form of consciousness, a transformation?

WS: Yes. Prayer certainly has to do with transformation. Transformation can only take place with a great effort, a commitment of time and knowledge. One transforms oneself from a captive of the associations of everyday life toward the highest energy, the indefinable.

P: Maybe we could consider prayer in the various traditions. It seems to me that there may be convergence as well as difference between the various traditions—the Buddhist, the Christian, the Jewish, the Islamic, the Hindu. . . .

WS: They are all related and all—all, I am certain—take into account the law of levels. No matter what the religion, at the highest level prayer is related and emerges as a state of silence, inner silence, inner stillness. At a very high level one may believe that one is having a dialogue or directing a petition to God. Still, even this prayer is related to the tangible—something which one can objectify. All prayer in all traditions converges.

This is emphasized in the *Hannya Shingyo,* the Buddhist Heart Sutra: "No prayer, no you, no me . . . no this, no that." It goes on until we come to "No thing. Nothing," where you can't put labels, you can't objectify. I think this view conceives of prayer as absolute emptiness, stillness.

P: How would you define the relationship between meditation and prayer?

WS: I think that perfect meditation could be termed perfect prayer. A person in a state of purity, in a state of prayer, would be a person in meditation. There are no associations, the mind and the body are stilled, open to a force which might be called God. This openness to Godliness may be where one arrives after a period of deepest prayer, and deepest meditation.

P: What is the effect on a human being of that contact, that experience?

WS: It could be called a state of absolute equilibrium, a balance of all parts of oneself. Most of us are in our heads or in our feelings for much of the time.

There is a knowledge and effectiveness in a person who's come to this balanced state: a realization that "You are I and I am YOU." There is no discrimination, no for or against; there is an acceptance of the "Is-ness" of things. One still sees the difference between the sparrow and the human being, but the man in this higher state is able to harmonize every aspect of himself.

P: In the Christian tradition that would be called charity or love.

WS: One has to love "being in a state of being" to love what is. To love one-self before being able to love a cat or God. To love is to be related to consciousness.

P: Can that come about through prayer? The love of oneself, the love of one's fellows, and the love of God seem to be a sequence.

WS: Yes, and the highest state is a progression toward being present—which means a silence, inward and outward. One is not apart from the inner silence.

P: What would you say are the optimum conditions for prayer?

WS: They would be a quiet place to sit, a relaxed erectness of posture, an awareness of breathing. One's body has to be relaxed, not tense. There should be a balance of the energies of the organism; the mind free of associations, the feelings quiet. A state of balance is essential.

P: How often and how long should one pray?

WS: There is an Islamic tale about Moses going to God to ask how many times a day people should pray. "A hundred," God answered, and Moses went back to his people, who told him, "It is impossible—go back and ask again." Moses went back and forth until God finally reduced the number to five. And so it has been for the Muslims ever since. For others it may be quite different. But regularity I would say is essential. A regular commitment to prayer. Of course, ideally one should be praying at every moment. There is neither night nor day if one is in a proper relationship to this silence. This goes on whether one is sleeping or waking.

P: Would that be the same as "practicing the presence"?

WS: I think that a person in a higher state, who is truly concentrating, would not be thinking about practicing anything. By his very being he will exert a beneficent effect on the world around him. He will not think of being of service—even that is a distraction—but no one will be of more use to humanity.

P: What about community, the presence of like-minded people?

WS: Certainly we can help each other. Your stillness helps me. If you are agitated, nervous, aggressive, you pull me down. We're helped by being with others who are like-minded. Compassion for others helps. Recall Shantideva's Bodhisattva vow:

May I be the doctor and the medicine;
And may I be the nurse
For all sick beings in the world
*Until everyone is healed.**

P: What about the rules, the commandments in the various traditions?

WS: Manifestations of greed, lust, cruelty. . . all these pull people down, drag them away from their reality. In all traditions the rules have to do with preventing that separation. In prayer one is free from the senses, from unworthy, unnecessary desires. The mind can be a help or a distraction.

P: Are there people in history or right now that are useful in terms of teaching us how to pray?

WS: Certainly there are many who can impart knowledge of right posture, right thinking, mindfulness, right attitude, and so on. Much knowledge can be passed on. The true objective of prayer is for people to know their true nature and by establishing themselves in this true nature to gain liberation. Much knowledge can be passed on, but the highest knowledge comes from oneself and is in oneself.

P: So the teacher is transitional?

WS: The guru or teacher can impart the principles relating to the importance of attention—to being present instead of distracted the way most people are. He or she can be an example, and impart lessons in being more awake, more attentive.

Prayer is here and now. The question of prayer is always concerned with the silence, the stillness.

P: What about the sacramental approach to life, ritual, thanksgiving, praise, adoration, etc., which we see in most traditions? How do they relate to prayer?

WS: I think they are all valuable in invoking higher energies. They all have their place on the spectrum of awareness, and they all help, but in the final analysis it comes down to what we were speaking of before, the Buddhist Heart Sutra: "No virtue, no evil, no this, no thing. Nothing." This is the state of pure being. It has nothing to do with helping or hurting others.

There may be certain steps to come to this place where I am God and God is me. We come to the state, the place where there's no thought of God,

*Translated from the Tibetan by Robert Thurman.

no reliance on anything but the listening to one's innermost presence, when mentation of any kind ceases. There is a giving up, a surrender of all the functional aspects of the body, but the body is still here. Levels of prayer range from the gambler at the racetrack who prays to win a sum of money to the one who is in a state of purity and awareness and is not moved by any thought or feeling.

Perhaps this is where the question of love comes in. One comes to this state not through wanting but through loving. One can't bear to be separated from the presence of this vibration; one wants always to be in the presence or related, a state of unwavering love.

P: So beyond willing is loving.

WS: Beyond desiring. Beyond all desire, except to be in a relationship to what we call God.

P: Is there a difference between the prayers of a young, a middle-aged, and an old man or woman?

WS: There must be a maturity which comes with old age; at the same time, the ardent wish which can help one towards the ultimate comes more with youth. I think there is an openness in children. Bhagavan Maharishi tells of a child who was asked, "Did you say your prayers?" The child answered, "I don't have to say my prayers; I'm going to sleep now. Sleep is my prayer." The Maharishi agreed with her. Sleep is prayer. When you are in a sleep state, you don't have any wish, you don't have any ambition. Close to sleep we are close to prayer. You realize that when you are soundly sleeping you are well off.

P: If you don't have bad dreams.

WS: Yes, but dreaming is not a sound sleep. When one is truly asleep, one is out—one has no associations. The mind is tranquil. One is in the prayerful sleep state that the child spoke about. When one wakes up, immediately thought comes in: "I want this." A desire comes in, an aggressive attitude, one is for or against something.

P: So you would say that the last thing you think before you go to sleep should be prayerful, as well as the first thing upon waking . . .

WS: . . . should be stillness. The last moments before you go to sleep should bring you to a state of relaxation in body and mind, an emptying of thoughts and feelings. In waking up one should again be aware of one's state of consciousness. An awareness persists however sleepy one is.

One's idea of prayer is most important. As we said, it can range from a wish for personal gain to a wish for contact with the highest.

P: William James says that prayer is the necessary core of religion: "Without prayer there is no religion."

WS: But aren't they the same thing? A coming together of the human and the highest—coming together with this vibration of Godliness. A definition of religion can be close to a definition of prayer. Otherwise it is a question of calling yourself a Sufi, a Jew, a Christian, a Hindu, a Buddhist—each has one concept of religion, but the highest religion would be a oneness within one-self and others.

P: You mentioned the Buddhist Heart Sutra as an ideal prayer. What would be the Jewish equivalent?

WS: I would say the *Shema*—"Hear O Israel, the Lord thy God is One"—is close to it. God is here, God is everywhere. There is no separation. Buddhism has many prayers that affirm the same truth in different words, even though there is no admission of the existence of God.

P: What about the Tibetan prayer at the time of death?

WS: What is advised by the Buddhists for the dying is a following of the light. And the following of the light requires an awareness, a being there. If there's fear, or a wish, one is not concentrated in one's attention towards the light; and it is this concentration and attention to the moment of dying that is important. One must be entirely present. No thinking about one's will, one's heirs, one's regrets.

P: Wouldn't that be the ultimate prayer, the consciousness of light?

WS: I don't know whether it is the *ultimate* prayer. It is very close to it, but when you say "consciousness of light," this is objectifying something, and for me in the ultimate prayer there would be no object, no light, no thing. So we are back to the Heart Sutra.

If we stop right now and are aware without being aware of any thing— that would be a very high state. As long as one objectifies, one hasn't reached the highest.

P: Would you say that prayer may be the principal means of knowing?

WS: We live in a very complex world. We don't know who we are, we don't un- derstand how our brain and our body function, we don't know who's guiding us, who is guiding the universe (in other words, who is running things)—we don't know any of that. But through prayer we might come to a state of knowing—not so much knowledge as knowing. An unknown knowing.

P: And well-being?

WS: Certainly prayer, as much as any human activity, can bring us that feeling of well-being, that conviction of Julian of Norwich that "all is well."

P: Is prayer the answer to the problem of evil?

WS: I think that prayer can diminish the amount of evil; though evil is also part of the scheme of things. It evidently has its place. We try to diminish it and to move towards a purity which is the opposite of evil. I think that prayer has this effect. There is Zen Roshi's claim that "sleeping beside the waterfall, I stopped the war." Sleep as prayer again. Without doing or wishing anything, it diminishes evil.

Gurdjieff said that by going into a church and by opening yourself, being aware, you can receive an energy which has been deposited by people in prayer. In a church, synagogue, temple, or any place where people have seriously launched prayer, the atmosphere is good. One benefits from the vibrations generated and deposited by others.

P: What about other aids to prayer? Rosaries, prayer wheels, walking, dancing, singing, chanting. . . .

WS: They are all aids. Good posture, a gesture can be an aid to prayer. You lift your hand in a certain gesture and immediately the turbulence, the impulses, and the agitations of the body are stilled. Dances, simple violent movements or smooth ones, like whirling—they all help to bring about concentration instead of diffusion of the energies within the organism. You can bring about a balance between different centers and parts of a human being. That can take years of training, and that is where a teacher comes in.

Almost every activity done with attention and presence can be a form of prayer. No matter what you are doing, if you do that with all your heart, and soul, and attention, it becomes a form of prayer which can lift you up.

P: That would include the arts.

WS: Absolutely. And crafts.

P: Can ritual be used to move one away from the "I want this . . . I want an answer" type of prayer?

WS: Ritual helps to prepare for prayer in its ultimate sense. Because the body and the mind do need preparation; the average person is distracted, manipulated—his body and his desires rule him. An evolved human being would have an inner intelligence which would understand that he's being worked on by many forces at many different levels. The seed of that true being which is prayer is in everyone. And ritual helps one to come close to it—to good morality. It helps to lift one. Prayer can lift us from level to level; we can't limit our idea of prayer.

Let us be still for a moment, and see if we can come to a prayerful state *now*. What would come out of being still and listening? Let's be quiet for just a moment. I wish to pray, to launch a prayer. What does it mean? What will it bring? How must I be? Am I able to pray? Am I fit? I need to calm my body, my mind, my emotions. As I speak with you I come closer to a relationship with another force; there is a greater sensitivity of the whole organism, an equilibrium. I'm not as taken with the noises of life. I've become a more intelligent, loving, even more poetical human being. I am not as distracted by that noise, the car alarm which is coming through the window. That sound is really useful: I am inviting hell into heaven.

Reaching for the Trapeze

An Interview with Peter Brook

From PARABOLA Vol. 15, No. 1, "Time & Presence"

Peter Brook is an internationally known film and theater director. His productions include **The Mahabharata, Meetings with Remarkable Men, Lord of the Flies, Marat/Sade, Conference of the Birds, A Midsummer Night's Dream,** and **The Cherry Orchard.**

PARABOLA: Our next two issues of the magazine will focus on the related themes of "Time & Presence" and "Attention." We see them as somewhat linked, because we feel that the only way one can begin to understand the vast subject of Time is through focusing on the present moment, and that the only way for one to be present in the moment is to have real attention or presence. And it seems perhaps this moment of presence relates very closely to the work of an actor. When an actor can have this kind of strong attention, in such a moment it seems he or she can actually transcend time and portray, for an audience, any time or place.

PETER BROOK: I think one of the subtle traps about this concept of being present is that whenever one searches for the "now," one gets the impression that the now has already disappeared, that one has just missed it. Non-time, or the "now," is this indescribable condition—I once heard an attempt to define it as the "flowing static."

In relation to the work of an actor, it's only when, by this curious and mysterious act of dissociating oneself, of separating oneself from the role, in the deepest way, that the actor can reach this core of non-image and non-time, out of which true acting manifestations can appear. And this is very rare. It's very difficult.

If you start at the outside, really at the most external level, with a bad actor—a beginner, a non-actor, say you or me, for example, trying to act—why, in fact, do we act badly? On one level because our body doesn't respond to what we ask it to do: our muscles and so forth aren't really under our control. But also, on a very simple level, there's a constant blurring and interference between two subjectivities meeting. There is the natural subjectivity of every person and one that an author has invented. And a great author's invented version is rich, it's real. So where the two meet, the result can only be like making a print by superimposing two totally different negatives. Take a negative of a radiant young girl, and print it on photographic enlarging paper, and then immediately superimpose another negative of a tense and hysterical woman onto it. And you have what happens when a bad actress tries to play Juliet.

P: But how does an actor or actress then reconcile these two subjectivities, these two times, without one distorting the other?

PB: The process then has to bring about an alignment of the two. It is not unlike what is implied in certain mystical traditions, which is the complete disappearance of the subjectivity of the actor. But that isn't exactly the case, because an actor doesn't really become an empty shell. There is something much finer, which is the interpenetration of the new subjectivity into an old, everyday subjectivity, which becomes more and more flexible, more and more spongelike, more transparent, until suddenly it accepts being like the wool taking on the color of the dye, to use an old Arabic image. It's very gradual, that dipping of the wool again and again into the dye until the whole texture is permeated.

And, in a way, the actor yields in the same gradual way, and the yielding is an opening by which he is, for a short time but very essentially, no longer just his subjectivity. So that what opens can be called his attention: an attention not clogged by imagery, not clogged by forms. Something in his deeper nature, without forms, begins to free itself inside this new structure, and right in the core of that there is a certain release from time. So that eventually what happens is that the greater the performer, the more there is a heightened sense of detail—which is what touches one in a performance, that beautifully alive sense of detail—coming from the fact that inside everything becomes slower and slower.

P: Could you elaborate a little on this connection between attention and timing? Surely it's not just actors that have this experience.

PB: I've observed this in three quite different areas of human performance. First, it has always fascinated me that when a trapeze artist leaps from one trapeze to another, the hand that reaches out to catch the other trapeze is actually quite slow. Whereas you and I would miss the trapeze because we grab too fast. You see it also in English cricket, which I was brought up on, where if you drop the ball, everyone jeers at you. But what actually happens is that when the ball comes sailing through the air, the person who catches it goes toward it very slowly. And the two come together. But when you try too hard, in a panic, you are always too fast.

The second observation that one can make easily is in classical ballet, which I find, in a way, is often a rather terrifying and ugly form. I once sat in a concert of the Bolshoi Ballet and realized that ninety-nine percent of the dancers were living in fear, because when they did these difficult pirouettes *en pointe* that they were forced to do, their emotion was not the joy of a dancer but the fear of not being with the last beat at the right moment—of not making it on time. But with the few great dancers, you have that extraordinary sense of watching them dance as though they may well be late, and because they are not afraid of being late, you see that their sense of timing becomes absolutely right.

The third example occurred when I was recently listening to a recording of Glenn Gould, and though he was in strict tempo, what gave a magic to each note was that you could hear that he went towards the note, not getting there a millionth of a second too soon. It was as though the tempo were simply there, and he just went toward it and arrived at the exact moment; so each measure rang with total satisfaction. There was never any grabbing, the way you see with most performers who are tense and try to grab the moment.

So this is one of the things that I continually stress with actors, that there is a link between these two kinds of time or tempo: that to be outwardly fast—quick and alert—is very related to an inner tempo where, right in the core, there is timelessness.

P: But surely one can be too slow, too? By not having any alertness or assurance, you could miss the trapeze or the ball or the beat just as easily. Doesn't this have a great deal to do with preparation—with being mentally and physically prepared for action?

PB: Of course, if one is really too slow, then one is not ready inside. It's a very curious thing. There is a kind of very ordinary lack of speed and timing which is simply the lack of all tension; in this there is no life whatsoever. Then there is what we are trying to speak of, which is a kind of non-speed or non-time, which is actually something that is beyond the ultimate speed and therefore is absolutely vibrant.

P: How can an actor use this sense of timing in his work?

PB: One has to recognize that today the actor is a tragic figure. Actors may have existed thousands of years ago in certain temples, where acting was inseparable from very, very high inner development. With this freedom came the capacity to enter into and play many roles. But today, this isn't the case. Actors are in a strange position—somewhat like fortune tellers, they are gifted with second sight, but that doesn't get them very far in their whole understanding and development, though it does give them the capacity to be lifted very temporarily to another level. Ninety percent of actors today will accept being actors on that basis, but there are some few actors who are interested in asking themselves what this means, and they have a tremendous capacity to evolve in a real evolutionary direction because they have a great gift.

P: Theater and film seem to have very different ways of approaching time. Since you directed *The Mahabharata* for both the stage and the screen, how did you deal with these different time states?

PB: That's interesting, because it touches on what I think is the real difficulty of filmmaking. When you work in the theater, you work toward the right tempo. There is always one true tempo, but it can't be fixed. So that in the lowest form of theater, you recognize that there is the necessity for everything on stage to be faster. So, when you come to Broadway, in a very practical sense, the director is simply getting people to move faster. A good commercial director is a man who, by shouting, by leaping on the stage, is driving it faster, and you get this famous thing of pace—has it got its pace?

Then there is another process, which is a little richer, where the true tempo arises through an evolving process which continues until the audience is confronted. In an acting performance that is really alive, everything is preparing the way, so that the tempo is never completely set but is very much contributed to by the audience. So when one says a true actor never repeats himself, it's not that he has to improvise broadly, but that he makes subtle changes in tempo so that nothing is ever the same twice.

Now in the cinema, the terrible difficulty is that there is no evolving process. The director alone, in a very short time, has to set the tempo, and the camera records it forever. This is terrifying, and very nearly impossible.

When I was doing my first film, I was told by John Huston that no matter how many films he had made, he always started shooting scenes at a pace that seemed fine to his ordinary eye, but then when he looked at them the next day, they were always too slow. And I've found it's absolutely true that whatever you do, watching the action with your naked eye, however much you try to put a frame of concentration around it, when you actually see it a day later, it's too slow.

It's very different from theater, where five seconds of an expressionless face can have a strong impact. But to see five seconds of an expressionless face in a movie is almost unbearable. About a hundredth of a second is about the most you can take of a frozen, expressionless face.

Therefore in a film, if a second has gone by and there isn't a new event, it's boring. What this means is that the director has to develop a very much heightened awareness in his watching. And since that seems virtually impossible, most filmmaking has to rely heavily on editing. I have seen films where the director tries for some sort of purist reason to do a scene in one long take, conceiving the whole shot like an exquisitely written line of verse which then can't be fiddled with, and very often the result is academic and cold. Because he has asked of himself something which only a Zen master could do.

P: So just being on this side of the camera and having tremendous attention to detail doesn't always work.

PB: No, because there is this whole question of the relation between the static and what is in movement. Once I took someone to see a really beautiful film, something very magical and aesthetic. And I was shocked that the person was completely bored. What I had forgotten was that within that aesthetic time, there also has to be that other tempo, the tempo of real life, which is a sort of vitality. The two always have to be present.

Very often within one form of aestheticism, one gets so taken with the detail that it carries with it the wrong form of slowness; or so captivated by energy and vitality that the finer energy is lost. What we're after is a marriage, always, between these two fields of energy, these two natures.

P: It must have been a tremendous task to take *The Mahabharata,* which you had spent a great deal of time putting into a nine-hour theatrical version, and condensing it so much further, into a three-hour film. Can you speak a bit about that process?

PB: There is also a six-hour version, for film and television. And I'm very interested that when it is shown in the cinema, we should show both versions. In the theater, there were some people who preferred the nine-hour marathon, all at one sitting, and others who preferred coming three separate evenings. There are people in the cinema who will respond to the six-hour version, and other people who will say, "No, I would never go to that, but I would go to a shorter version." As in India, where various lengths of publication—and performance—of *The Mahabharata* exist. There are a large number of versions in India, as there are in the English-speaking world as well. There are about twenty two- to three-hundred page versions, which is what most people actually prefer. There are very few people who have read the complete work, which is some seventeen volumes.

I really didn't want to make the shorter film version at first, but I was persuaded to and accepted in the end willingly, on the grounds that, like the shortened book version, in this concentrated form, a taste is given. An essential taste can come through it. But if you pay the price of giving up six hours, you are more than doubly rewarded. The one thing we haven't cut by one word from the longer screen version is the *Gita*.

P: As I recall, on stage the message of the *Bhaghavad-Gita* section from the epic was simply whispered. Why in the film did you decide to dramatize it?

PB: The stage version came out of genuine respect on the part of the playwright, Jean-Claude Carrière, and myself. In the theater, one has to admit the limitations of the form, and our sense was that the *Gita* is a teaching too intimate, too special, to be put onto any stage. And we were simply being respectful. Rather than do a digest, which we thought would be cheapening it, we hit upon this idea of showing the audience that this is a mystery by having it whispered. And leaving it up to them to discover what was said.

But we were much criticized for that, rather unexpectedly. And I read things that I really took notice of. I got letters, people saying, "Why did you deliberately take the teaching out of it?" or "Why were you afraid to let this in?" And this worried me. I felt this a total misunderstanding if it looks as though this is a view that is so modern and so Western that the *Gita* is ignored. So we began to be very concerned by that.

Then I came back to the fact that after all one can't say that the *Gita* is a secret and hidden temple teaching that you are violating if you put it in the marketplace, because after all every word of it is right out in the open. It was never originally given to an esoteric group. It wasn't even Christ teaching just to his disciples. It was already in the marketplace.

And then we began seeing that in the cinema, you do have a new possibility. The *Gita,* a teaching like that, which is man to man, has to be projected loud if you're playing in a big space like the Majestic in Brooklyn or in an open-air quarry. You can't do it quietly. You have to do it fake quietly. But in the cinema, it was quite clear that you could touch the reality of it. It could still be very personal. It can be, just as the story dictates.

And that story is about people waiting for an endless time. Time stops on this battlefield, for maybe days, without anybody realizing that they're waiting. The teaching goes on. You can time the real *Gita* and see how long those armies had to wait.

P: There's a tremendous sense of intimacy—and certainly of presence—in that scene in the film. You've spoken at other times about the particular difficulties of filming this project—the large cast and crew—and the pressures of doing the project on a tight budget with too little time to develop each scene fully, the way it had been more possible on the stage. How is it that this scene worked so effectively?

PB: The day we did the *Gita,* by a miraculous series of events, there were very few people on the set. No horses, no electricians yelling at each other and rushing the cameramen, none of the absolute nightmare that had marked most of the productions on the sound stage.

Instead, on that day, there were very few people around. Most of those who had been there earlier were absorbed in preparing other things, or were not actually needed. So we had a day when there was absolute quiet and concentration. Which was exactly what was necessary. And so, the *Gita* in the film is the result of that particular time and those particular conditions.

The Command Is to Hear

An Interview with Rabbi Adin Steinsaltz

From PARABOLA Vol. 19, No. 1, "The Call"

Rabbi Adin Steinsaltz, an Israeli-born scholar, teacher, mathematician, chemist, botanist, linguist, sculptor, and Biblical zoologist, is the author of numerous books and articles on Jewish philosophy and mysticism.

PARABOLA: The call is a very great mystery. Could it be said that God's call is a call to be here, present, in the moment? Is this why Abraham, Jacob, Moses, Isaiah all answered the voice of God with the same words: "Here am I," "I am here," as if the call was meant as a call to Be, to be the "I am"?

ADIN STEINSALTZ: The "I am" is sometimes as if you were answering "Hello" on the telephone. "I am here" in many ways just says "I am listening." The call is directed and not directed, it goes everywhere, in every time, and never stops— but most people don't hear it. When you hear the call, you say, "I'm here." Just imagine a person sitting on a star, sending messages to other planets; he's sending messages over and over. Now what will be the break-through point? The breakthrough point is when there is *any* answer. When at the end of nowhere, somebody answers.

P: You mean the voice is always sounding?

AS: Yes, but we are not listening. It even says so in the Bible. It is written that the voice on Sinai was a mighty voice that did not stop. Many years later this is repeated in much of the Hasidic literature, that the voice giving the Law, the Ten Commandments, never stopped. It is still giving the Law for ever and ever, for eternity. Put in another way, there is a very clear message that is always being transmitted. The thing that has changed is that we are no longer listening.

P: And the command is, "Hear, O Israel."

AS: The command is, first of all, to hear. If you don't hear the *Shema Israel*, where are you? So you must first hear. Now, if you are listening, and answer, "Here I am. I am listening," then perhaps a message can come through.

P: The Talmud says: "If you listen below, you will deserve to hear from above." So is it a question of our attention?

AS: Yes. It is a question of our attention. I once wrote about it. There's a saying in the Talmud that there are voices which are so resonant, they should be heard all over the world. One of them is the voice of a woman giving birth, and another is the voice of a snake getting out of its skin. These voices should be heard, but why aren't they? Because the voice of Rome, the voice of the big, busy city, has so much power, it obliterates them.

P: But what of a heavenly voice?

AS: It's what I'm saying. The voice of Rome obliterates almost everything. So the real point is about listening, not so much about the voice.

P: When the voice calls, why is the name always repeated? God says, "Abraham, Abraham," "Moses, Moses," "Jacob, Jacob." Is there a meaning to this?

AS: I suppose that it's possible that one time is not enough. It is like shaking somebody who's asleep. At a deeper level, the double call is uplifting, causing the person to move from one level (the name) of his existence to a higher level of the same person. In the Bible, in the first prophecy of Samuel, he hears a voice, but he thinks that it's something else. He needs to wake up. The waking up is a process, and it's a process that has to go through different levels. On one level—again, a quote from the Talmud—"Every day there is a voice coming from Mount Sinai that says 'Repent, errant children!'" Now the Baal Shem Tov is quoted as saying, "There is a basic question: if there is such a voice, why don't I hear it? Or if it is a voice that is not heard, why say it?" And his answer was that those thoughts that come to a person from nowhere somehow call him to repent, to change something in his life. These are the echoes of the voice.

P: Can the hearer know whether the voice is the voice of God, or whether the voice is the voice of an angel?

AS: This is basically what I would call the human problem. You see, the divine problem is to call. The human problem is to know who is calling. You find it throughout the Bible and later, the constant question: whose voice is it? Because some people think that the mere fact of having a supernatural, parapsychological experience is meaningful. But such an experience is just that: a parapsychological experience, and that's the end of it. Merely hearing voices does not mean that one has heard the voice of God, and that is always the big temptation and the downfall of quite a number of people. There are some who are cheats, meaning people who never had an experience, and are just imitating. But there are many people who really heard something, and their very big mistake was that they didn't identify the voice. There is another Biblical quotation: when Gideon has his experience, he hears a voice, and he says, "God, how shall I know that *you* are speaking to me?" This is in many ways the most pertinent question. "Give me a sign that it is You who are speaking to me" (Judges 6:17).

P: It's an accepted teaching that Muhammad was called by an angel, not by God. What is the role of angels?

AS: We usually say that it depends on the degree. Some people hear a voice directly. Some people hear a voice of an angel. And some people don't even hear that. You know, in Jewish parlance, we speak about something which is called *bat kol*. Bat kol means an echo, but it is not an echo of the mountains. Translated literally it means "daughter of a voice." You don't hear the voice itself, you hear only the child of the voice. You don't hear the origin of the voice, you hear it only on the second level. In the Book of Isaiah, in one of the prophesies about the future, it says, "And you shall hear a voice behind you, telling you go left or go right." Now this is a voice, but some people don't hear it. They hear what they call an echo, a daughter of a voice. It was again written that in the time of the First Temple, people got calls directly. The prophets of the time of the Second Temple all talked with angels. Later on, we don't hear the voice any more; instead we have the bat kol, the daughter of the voice.

P: And that becomes—again, according to the Talmud—the sole means of communication between God and humans.

AS: Yes, that is the sole means of communication which is directed to a single person or to many people. Sometimes this echo becomes thinned.

P: How do you prepare to receive the echo?

AS: Having the call at this level is a very great achievement, even if you hear the echo—even if you hear, so to speak, the echo of the echo. In quite recent times, there was a Hasidic rabbi who said that in order for a person to be, not just a leader, but a guide of people, he has to have a *ruah hakodesh*, a holy spirit. He added, at least he should have an unconscious holy spirit. According to this rabbi, some people have a kind of a clarity of vision; they know how the vision comes and what it says. There are others who don't have that clarity, what they will see doesn't depend on them; they are so-to-say guided unknowingly.

P: There are many different ways that the call can be received: an angel spoke to Jacob in a dream, Ezekiel felt a hand on his shoulder. What are the different forms the call can take?

AS: We never know. One also has to remember that not everyone who has been called is telling us. Sometimes people get not just a call, but also a message. Sometimes the call may be completely personal, so it's nobody else's business. How the call comes, from the descriptions we have received, is by means of what it is that makes a person attentive. It can be visual, auditory, it can be tactile, or it can be any other way that the person has of knowing.

P: What is the effect of the call? Does a change, an awakening, a reorientation occur?

AS: I suppose that most of these calls, like God's appearance in the world, leave it for me—for the other side—to act. And usually, I don't think that the call really changes what I would call my free will.

P: But surely when one feels something from above and is touched by it in some way, one must be changed.

AS: Even when there is a change, it depends on how deep and how clear the message is. As I say, sometimes it comes loud and clear, and sometimes it comes in a much more clouded way, and sometimes a person doesn't even know. A person may receive a very clear message without knowing it; sometimes events, life, or things converge upon a person, but that person doesn't recognize that he is being called. You may have more than one call. Sometimes the call comes not through any kind of a voice; sometimes the call comes because you are put into a position in which a choice is made for you which you never imagined. It may begin from anything—from an accident to a disaster. And it may come through a chance meeting. Sometimes you ask a question at large, and you receive a very clear answer when the person who answered it, who was the instrument for answering it, didn't ever know that he was giving you an answer. So I'm saying that the change, whatever the change is, seems to be that there is something which I now know. I know at a certain level that I am being told something. What I'm doing with it is a completely different thing. It could even be that I will ignore it.

P: There's a whole history of people who refuse the call. Jonah fled.

AS: Yes, people refuse the call in different ways. Somebody said a prophet can refuse the call, but he will pay for it with his life. In Ezekiel there is the parable of the watchman who has to warn the people. Now, what happens if he doesn't give the warning? If he tries to flee, or tries to ignore it, later he may pay for it very heavily.

P: At the same time that God is addressing us, we are addressing God. Is prayer our side of the dialogue, or is there something else?

AS: Well, prayer is clearly meant to be something like this. I'm very busy these days finishing a book about the *Siddur* [prayer book], a big book that will appear in English. One of the things that I say is that prayer is basically a kind of very direct talk. Prayer is "I am telling you," and this is something that changes. Some prayers or blessings are just a few words saying, "Thank you. I just want to say thank you," nothing else. In some prayers, I ask something. In others I just complain: "It's not just, it's not fair. You dealt with me wrongly." All of these are prayers, and they can move from a feeling of bliss to a feeling of extreme anger.

P: When we pray, who is listening?

AS: The fact that God is listening is no wonder. We want also, from time to time, to get some kind of a sign that at least our prayer has been received. I remember this feeling. It is like the times that I've been left alone in a radio booth. The people trust me that I won't botch it, so they go out for tea and leave me alone to broadcast. Then I feel: I am talking; is anybody listening? I want at least to get some kind of a notion that somebody is listening. As there is a command from the one side—*Shema Israel,* "Hear, O Israel"—so there is a petition from the other side in the book of Psalms, or the prayer book—"Hear me. God, hear me, listen to me." I want to know that somebody is hearing. As it is, except for perhaps a few people throughout history, nobody has this kind of an immediate response, the feeling that the message has been received. I'm not speaking about being answered favorably, I'm speaking about the message being received at the other end.

P: How can we be better receivers?

AS: We are not always well equipped for receiving. I hear a call, and I'm not equipped. Let's take this room for example. On a completely physical level, this room is full of voices and images. If I have a radio receiver I'll hear voices, and if I have a television receiver I'll see images. So the images are here, the voices are here. They are all over me, they are overwhelming, but I don't see or hear them. But not everyone is so closed. A Hasidic rabbi once said that he was praying to have the voices a little bit dulled. He couldn't rest, he couldn't sleep, because he was hearing voices all the time. He was distraught from having a very broad range receiver.

P: Is there a finer energy that can connect us to a current of life from which the call from above comes?

AS: I have always been very, very suspicious about finding artificial means—it doesn't really matter whether it is a mantra or a drug. Do you know that book by Aldous Huxley about the gates of heaven and hell? One of his basic points (which I think was a mistake) was that he thought that somehow he had found the key to another realm. That was the basic notion, and he wrote very beautifully about it. Now, as more and more people that tried it found out, you don't get a gateway to heaven. You get, at the most, a gateway into another chamber within yourself.

P: Isn't what we are searching for within ourselves?

AS: No, that is not the real search. We may have wonderful experiences and clearly have within us more than we know or more than the eye catches, but we're trying to pass over and through self to the Other. Now I may find out lots of beautiful things or horrible things within my microcosms, and there may be ways and means and exercises to get there, but the real problem is that this is still my own realm, and I want really to go to the Other Side. There are, I think somewhere in the States, a few miles of receiving antennas that are meant specifically to receive calls from outer space. Just imagine that you receive a message—you are overjoyed. You hear a voice, and it's coming from a very small transmitter on the other side of the earth. It's a wonderful discovery, but that wasn't what you were searching for. You were searching for something from the other side of nowhere. You didn't want to find something within your realm.

P: The sound of the *shofar* in synagogue on Rosh Hashanah seems to be a call. So in a sense the call doesn't have to come from another world. There's a certain sound of another world in the shofar. There's a reminder in it, an awakener.

AS: Yes, but it is like getting a beep before the news. That is what it says: it's no news, it's just the beep telling you, I'm here tuned to the news.

P: But at least it's a reminder.

AS: In many ways the religious life is supposed to be a reminder. Now, as it happens, people get accustomed even to the reminder. The alarm clock is ringing and you go on sleeping. You become so accustomed to these calls that you sleep through them, and just weave them into your dream.

P: What could be an awakener?

AS: If I may quote the Almighty, he says in the book of Deuteronomy: "Who will make them, or lead them, who will make them listen to me as they are listening to me now, that their heart will be ready for me as it is now?" But people are not always willing to repeat this experience because hearing such a voice is a terrible burden, it is always a shocking thing to have, so the notion of delegating it comes from a desire to protect myself from that pain, from the too-big experience. People are willing to have small adventures, small thrills, and small frights. But how many shocks can I have? Sometimes one is enough for a lifetime, I don't want to repeat it. Sometimes you have experiences that you want to repeat, but you just don't get the chance, and sometimes one is more than enough; it has been great, important, stirring— but one does not wish to go through it again. Some experiences are such that, if it is a real voice that has been heard, it is always connected and involved with either pain or very great suffering; what is called a dark, big fear is a part of it. You can see in the Biblical descriptions of the prophet, it is really suffering.

P: Are you saying that we need to suffer?

AS: I am not speaking about the need to suffer as cleansing, I am speaking about how the experience of getting such a transmission is on its own a very painful one, and that is why people subconsciously shy away from it.

P: At the same time—the call is maybe another word for grace, and we have the written experience of many people whose lives have been transformed by this touch from above.

AS: Let me put it this way: there are some people that are blessed. They get a blessing, but they do not always get a call. To get a blessing, is, in a certain way, a passive experience, and to hear a voice is a listening experience. This kind of listening, an active listening, demands a great effort from the listener.

P: When PARABOLA interviewed you for the "Wholeness" issue [Vol. X, No. 1, 1985], you said, "One of the first conditions is to listen. He is speaking all the time. The voice doesn't stop; we just stopped hearing. It isn't a phenomenon in time, but a phenomenon in eternity. It is our work to be ready to do the listening."

AS: So I didn't change that much!

P: It seems that really the most important thing for us is to listen.

AS: To be able to listen.

P: But how do we learn to hear?

AS: We don't learn to hear. The only thing that we can really learn is that something may happen, and when it comes, listen. In the first revelation to Moses, he is not sure what has happened; he has to be given some kind of sign. There's an immediate call to see a sign, the burning bush, just in order to come close, which is again the same thing: it's like knocking on the door, like feeling a hand on your shoulder. It's not in itself a message, but it is a kind of awakening. Moses hears it. The Midrash says that later, Moses says to God, "Reveal yourself to me." And God says, "You cannot see my face . . . I will cover you and you will see something anyway." And the Midrash says that God told Moses: "When I wanted it, you didn't want it. You hid your face. When you want it, I don't want it." Sometimes the only thing to be learned is this: when the call comes, jump!

The Experience of Change

An Interview with H. H. the Dalai Lama

From PARABOLA Vol. 15, No. 1, "Time & Presence"

Born in northeastern Tibet, **Tenzin Gyatso** is the fourteenth Dalai Lama, the spiritual leader of Tibetan Buddhists worldwide. He left his native country in 1959, during the Tibetan uprising against Chinese Communist rule, which was imposed in 1950. His headquarters are now in Dharamsala, India. This interview took place shortly before he was awarded the Nobel Peace Prize in 1989.

Daniel Goleman covers behavioral and brain sciences for **The New York Times.** He is the author of **The Meditative Mind** (Tarcher) and **Emotional Intelligence** (Bantam).

DANIEL GOLEMAN: PARABOLA is trying to look at the question of time from many points of view, and we want to ask you for the Buddhist understanding of it. How can we relate our sense of the process of time to our experience of the present moment? Time passes and yet the moment seems fixed in an eternal present.

HIS HOLINESS THE DALAI LAMA: In Buddhism, the concept of linear time, of time as a kind of container, is not accepted. Time itself, I think, is something quite weak—it depends on some physical basis, some specific thing. Apart from that thing it is difficult to pinpoint—to see time. Time is understood or conceived only in relation to a phenomenon or a process.

DG: Yet the passage of time seems very concrete—the past, the present, aging. The process of time seems very real.

HH: This business of time is a difficult subject. There are several different explanations and theories about time; there is no one explanation in Buddhism. I feel there is a difference between time and the phenomena on which time is projected. Time can be spoken of only in relation to phenomena susceptible to change, which because they are susceptible to change are transitory and impermanent. "Impermanent" means there is a process. If there is no process of change, then one cannot conceive of time in the first place.

The question is whether it is possible to imagine an independent time which is not related to any particulars, any object that goes through change. In relation to such an object, we can talk about the past of that thing, its present state, and its future; but without relation to such particulars, it is very difficult to conceive of an instant of time totally independent of a particular basis.

DG: Can we connect what you are saying with our own experience? We experience time, we experience growth and aging, we experience that one thing leads to another.

HH: That's right.

DG: One thing is the cause of another thing. Now how do we explain that process of time in terms of being in the present moment? There are differences in the way each of us experiences time. Sometimes it goes very slowly, sometimes very quickly. Our sense of time seems to change with our state of consciousness. If you're fully focused—just right here, right now—then the sense of time changes. What is the relationship between the sense of time and one's own state of consciousness?

HH: Depending on a person's spiritual maturity or realization, there could be a difference in how one sees the moment. That one could have different experiences of time is demonstrated by an ordinary fact: For instance, if two people attend a party, one person might be so absorbed in the party he would feel that time went (*snaps his fingers*) just like that! Whereas the other person who did not enjoy it very much might have felt it long, dragging, because he was thinking about when it would finish. So although both of them attended the same party, in terms of time they were different.

DG: Let's say one's life is like that party. How can one perhaps use paying a fuller attention to the moment to expand a sense of time or to more fully enjoy the part that is one's life? Does cultivating attention play a role in this?

HH: It does play a great role. If you have more attentiveness, if you have a fuller sense of presence, then it will make a great deal of difference in how you experience your life.

But then, you find that if you analyze time very precisely, there is no present, in the real sense of the word; only past and future, no present! The sense of present that we have is a conventional notion. Even if you employ a computer or some other instrument to divide time and analyze whether there was a present or not, you would find that there isn't. "Present" is a relative term. While in experience there seems to be nothing but the present, we actually experience only the illusion of the present.

Things are all the time moving, never fixed. So we can't find the present. This fact indicates the impermanent, dynamic nature of things, that they never remain fixed or static, they are always in the process of changing from one form to another.

DG: But isn't it possible to be present in that movement—with attention?

HH: Attention—yes! That's present! And present, you see, makes past and future. Without present, you can't posit future and past.

DG: Conceptually this is very upsetting, you know; that's fine, that's okay, but . . . (*Much laughter. His Holiness is delighted*) . . . but now that you've upset my concepts, I've got to clarify this. You're saying that if you're totally present in the moment, fully attentive to the moment, the mind is attending not to a "present," but rather a future becoming a past. Is that right? That seems to follow from what you say—that in a certain state of full awareness what you see is change, simply change: the future becoming the past. Is that the case? What you are really saying is that we don't experience time at all; we experience change.

HH: Yes! My point is not to deny the existence of the present, but rather the present independent of some object that changes. If we investigate, the present is very difficult to find, but that does not mean the present does not exist. But when you talk about the concept of time, it creates confusion, because it is not based in matter. We could try to talk objectively of time as it is based in matter: anything made of matter goes through a process of change from moment to moment. Within a minute, within seconds, within one hundredth of a second, it is all the time changing. It can be spoken of only in terms of something that is subject to change. There is no independent, linear time as some kind of container.

DG: Could we talk about that experience, then? (*laughter*)

HH: The experience of change. . . . Yesterday I was talking to some neuroscientists about how difficult it is to say what consciousness is! On this planet there are something like five billion human beings, so there are five billion perceptions of reality. Everyone can be looking at the same object, but seeing it very differently.

DG: The person who has the better time at the party—is it that that person is more aware of impermanence?

HH: It hasn't so much to do with awareness of impermanence, but rather with a very instinctive nature of humans, which is that we lack contentment. When we enjoy something, we feel it has gone very fast. We are not satisfied, we want more. When we do not desire a particular experience, then that situation seems very long.

DG: In modern life, there is a disease called "time sickness." Time sickness is the sense that there's never enough time, that time is passing too quickly. With it comes anxiety about what's going to happen. Fear and anxiety seem to be related to wanting to stop change, wanting to hold on to time. What is the cure for time sickness?

HH: One cure is to reduce the dependence on machines! Time is moving, moving, so we feel we have to catch up. . . .

DG: Catch up with the pace of technology?

HH: I think that is the problem. But that doesn't seem practical!

DG: If you have to live with machines, then what can you do?

HH: Machines are okay. It is our attitude. Attitudes toward them play a great role. Generally speaking, the original idea of inventing these technologies was to serve humanity; so if you are able to retain that kind of attitude toward technology, then you will be able to command technology to do what you want, and if you find the pace of machines too fast, to stop.

DG: To turn them off?

HH: To change one's attitude. It is by their dependence that humans give technology the upper hand.

DG: All of society is slave to this pace of technology, so if you're to live in society, you can't just turn it off. Is there anything you can do inside to control this anxiety?

HH: There's a big difference one could make by changing one's attitude. Although the situation might be such that you are pressed to do something, due to your way of looking at things you might even be able to reduce that tension you would normally have otherwise. Through training of the mind, discipline of the mind, one could really reduce the anxiety that is usually associated with being pressed.

In some cases you see people who are very rushed. But they still handle the situation very slowly and very powerfully. In another case, the person remains anxious all the time, even during holidays!

DG: It's a very big problem in modern society, an epidemic. Is there any particular remedy? What is the quality of mind a person needs to be free of it?

HH: A lot of factors might be at play, depending on what mental attitude you have toward certain things and how you deal with it. In some people, according to the Tibetan medical system, it is due to an inner imbalance in the body that makes the person very nervous. In that case you need a treatment of the body. And in some cases the body's condition is very normal, yet the person is anxious. Each case is different and there's a different technique for overcoming it. Generally speaking, I think peace of mind plays a major role in this. Basically, the person whose mind is calm and easy, who is a giving person, has things go more easily when there's some difficulty in the situation.

DG: Then time is manageable.

HH: Oh, yes.

DG: Is there a relationship between the sense of time and cultivating patience or even forgiveness? Does your sense of time have something to do with that?

HH: There is a connection. If you are able to understand the dynamic process in the changing nature of situations, events, and things, then your tolerance and patience can offset the difficulties.

DG: What this brings to mind is the historical urgency about the situation in Tibet, and the repression there by the Chinese. I'm struck by your ability to be so forgiving and patient. Is it because of your sense of time, of a larger historical perspective?

HH: It does play a role in the sense that the fate of a nation is a question of generations or of centuries, not a question of months or years. And realizing that fact, you see that something that is happening now is the consequence of something that has taken place over a long period of time.

It's not so much an understanding of time, but an understanding of reality, of the forces contributing to such and such events and how they are beyond the control of the present generation. Knowing these factors plays a role in reducing the feeling of frustration.

One thing that influences my outlook is that if in any situation there is no solution, there is no point in being anxious. If the forces at work have their own momentum, and what's going on now is the product of what went before, and this generation is not in control of all those forces, then this process will continue.

DG: So you are patient with it because of that larger perspective—you mentioned centuries, not just generations.

HH: If there is no way out, there is no point in wasting time in worrying.

I would like to talk a little about the question of attitude in how to overcome time sickness. From a Buddhist point of view, the realization of understanding of the nature of *samsara* applies. You know, it's very bad in Tibet—an independent country occupied—there's lots of trouble and it will remain for some time. So long as the human community is also under the influence of ignorance, some sort of trouble will always be there. But there's another thing: if there is trouble, some understanding brings a benefit from it. Life becomes useful, when you confront a difficulty; it provides a kind of value for your life to have the kind of responsibility to confront it and overcome it. Whereas if you do not feel such difficulties, there's no such responsibility, no role for you to play in your life.

DG: No meaning.

HH: No meaning, yes. That challenge allows you to practice your ability. Basically, the purpose of life is to serve other people, to do something of benefit for other people. From that point of view, a difficulty is really a great opportunity. I have often said that our generation of Tibetans is seeing the saddest period in all of Tibetan history. So from that angle it is, how do you say, very unfortunate; but at the same time, as bad as it is, in another sense it's a great honor, a great privilege, you see?—to face these times, to confront them. That is the opportunity to show the Tibetan nation's ability. So it's a great honor.

Although it's very difficult to actually find what consciousness and mind are, it is these different ways of looking at things and how it influences your experience of them that shows the elasticity of mind, of consciousness.

DG: What I'm struck by in what you're saying is that one's perspective, one's view of things, determines how time is experienced—how one experiences change, life, and the purpose of life—whether life is empty or full. And it's not the specifics of the situation, it's how you see it. And I suppose that applies to time, too.

HH: Yes, yes, that's good. But it does also depend on external circumstances, and how the two come together.

DG: But if you have a view of lifetime after lifetime, of reincarnation and trying to help sentient beings, does that lead you to give more importance or less importance to the present moment?—I know, of course, that we've established the present moment doesn't exist! (*laughter*) But the English language hasn't caught up with your thinking!

HH: Of course, even if you see only one lifetime, it's the same as if you see many births, many lives. If there are many unfortunate things in your life, or if you have had a much happier life with many good opportunities, you still want one hundred years of life.

You see, the past is past, and the future is yet to come. That means the future is in your hands—the future entirely depends on the present. That realization gives you a great responsibility.

DG: One way most people are concerned about time is how long they will live. But what about the bardo state? In the West, we think of death as a discontinuous event: you're alive and then you're dead. It seems from the Buddhist point of view that dying is a process—there's a continuity as you change from one state of existence to another.

HH: Yes.

DG: How long does this process take, going from this one state, life, to the other, death?

HH: It's quite indefinite. For some people it can be as short as five minutes; I think the quickest would be within seconds. But there is quite a difference. When we talk about time now, we're talking in terms of human understanding of it. However, I think time with matter and time with consciousness, again, are entirely different. So you see, time with the rough body and time with the subtle body—it is not the same.

DG: You mean the frame of time is different?

HH: Yes. So for beings in the intermediate state [the bardo], from their point of view there is maybe time to do things—to evolve, to go through the process of dying and so on. But from the ordinary human point of view, it could be just a momentary instant.

DG: You mean that within an ordinary human instant, from another point of view there's a vast amount of time?

HH: A time which from one perspective may appear as momentary, from another perspective can appear very long.

DG: It's like in physics, where the physical laws outside the atom differ from quantum principles within the atom. You're saying something parallel happens with time. From a human point of view, let's say time acts akin to Newtonian physics, and seems very quick. But from another point of view— the subtle body, which is a consciousness not based on physical matter—it's like quantum mechanics, and the same instant can be very long. Is that so? Are there different kinds of time?

HH: Yes, that's possible. Depending on how advanced your level of mind is, your perception of time changes. Something that ordinarily appears as momentary may appear very long. And as you're dying, there can be both normal time and this expanded time. As you shift to the subtle body, time expands. Consciousness is not tied down by the physical body. For the subtle body, things can move faster than the speed of light. There are two kinds of time: physical time and inner time.

In Buddhism, there are many realms, each with its own scale of time. There are infinite universes and infinite time scales.

Over Twenty-five Years of PARABOLA *Back Issues*

VOL. 1   No. 1:   **The Hero** - In quest of the meaning of Self
        No. 2:   **Magic** - The power that transforms
        No. 3:   **Initiation** - A portal to rebirth
        No. 4:   **Rites of Passage** - Symbols and rituals of transformation

VOL. 2   No. 1:   **Death** - Beyond the limits of the known
        No. 2:   **Creation** - From out of formlessness, something new
        No. 3:   **Cosmology** - The order of things, seen and unseen
        No. 4:   **Relationships** - Our interwoven human experience

VOL. 3   No. 1:   **Sacred Space** - Landscapes, temples, the inner terrain
        No. 2:   **Sacrifice & Transformation** - Stepping into a holy fire
        No. 3:   **Inner Alchemy** - Refining the gold within
        No. 4:   **Androgyny** - The fusion of male and female

VOL. 4   No. 1:   **The Trickster** - Guide, mischief-maker, master of disguise
        No. 2:   **Sacred Dance** - Moving to worship, moving to transcend
        No. 3:   **The Child** - Setting out from innocence
        No. 4:   **Storytelling & Education** - Speaking to young minds

VOL. 5   No. 1:   **The Old Ones** - Visions of our elders
        No. 2:   **Music, Sound, & Silence** - Echoes of stillness
        No. 3:   **Obstacles** - In the way, or the Way itself?
        No. 4:   **Woman** - In search of the feminine

VOL. 6   No. 1:   **Earth & Spirit** - Opposites or complements?
        No. 2:   **The Dream of Progress** - Our modern fantasy
        No. 3:   **Mask & Metaphor** - When things are not as they seem
        No. 4:   **Demons** - Spirits of the dark

VOL. 7   No. 1:   **Sleep** - To be restored, or to forget
        No. 2:   **Dreams & Seeing** - Visions, fantasy, and the unconscious
        No. 3:   **Ceremonies** - Seeking divine service
        No. 4:   **Holy War** - Conflict for the sake of reconciliation

VOL. 8   No. 1:   **Guilt** - The burden of conscience
        No. 2:   **Animals** - The nature of the creature world
        No. 3:   **Words of Power** - Secret words, magic spells, divine utterances
        No. 4:   **Sun & Moon** - Partners in time as fields of force

VOL. 9   No. 1:   **Hierarchy** - The ladder of the sacred
        No. 2:   **Theft** - The paradox of possession
        No. 3:   **Pilgrimage** - Journey toward the holy
        No. 4:   **Food** - Nourishing body and spirit

VOL. 10   No. 1:   **Wholeness** - The hunger for completion
        No. 2:   **Exile** - Cut off from the homeland of meaning
        No. 3:   **The Body** - Half dust, half deity
        No. 4:   **The Seven Deadly Sins** - The mystery of goodness

VOL. 11   No. 1:   **The Witness** - Silents guides and unsleeping eyes
          No. 2:   **Mirrors** - That which reflects the real
          No. 3:   **Sadness** - The transformation of tragedy
          No. 4:   **Memory & Forgetting** - What we remember and why

VOL. 12   No. 1:   **The Knight & the Hermit** - Heroes of action and reflection
          No. 2:   **Addiction** - The prison of human craving
          No. 3:   **Forgiveness** - The past transcended
          No. 4:   **The Sense of Humor** - Walking with laughter

VOL. 13   No. 1:   **The Creative Response** - To represent the sacred
          No. 2:   **Repetition & Renewal** - Respecting the rhythm of growth
          No. 3:   **Questions** - The road to understanding
          No. 4:   **The Mountain** - A meeting place of Earth and Heaven

VOL. 14   No. 1:   **Disciples & Discipline** - Teachers, masters, students, fools
          No. 2:   **Tradition & Transmission** - Passages from wisdom into wisdom
          No. 3:   **The Tree of Life** - Root, trunk, and crown of our search
          No. 4:   **Triad** - Sacred and secular repetitions of the law of three

VOL. 15   No. 1:   **Time & Presence** - How to welcome the present moment
          No. 2:   **Attention** - The mysterious force that animates mind, body, and feeling
          No. 3:   **Liberation** - Freedom from what, freedom for what?
          No. 4:   **Hospitality** - Care in human relationships

VOL. 16   No. 1:   **Money** - Exchange between humans, and with the divine
          No. 2:   **The Hunter** - Stalking great knowledge
          No. 3:   **Craft** - The skill that leads to creation
          No. 4:   **The Golden Mean** - Balance between defect and excess

VOL. 17   No. 1: **Solitude & Community** - The self, alone and with others
          No. 2: **Labyrinth** - The path to inner treasure
          No. 3: **The Oral Tradition** - Transmission through spoken word & silence
          No. 4: **Power & Energy** - The stunning array of atom and cosmos

VOL. 18   No. 1: **Healing** - The return to a state of health
          No. 2: **Place & Space** - Seeking the holy in mountain, sea, and vale
          No. 3: **Crossroads** - The meeting place of traditions, cultures, ideas
          No. 4: **The City** - Hub of the human world

VOL. 19   No. 1: **The Call** - To ask for help, to receive what is given
          No. 2: **Twins** - The two who come from one
          No. 3: **Clothing** - Concealing and revealing our inner selves
          No. 4: **Hidden Treasure** - Value, hope, and knowledge

VOL. 20   No. 1: **Earth, Air, Water, Fire** - Essential elements of all things
          No. 2: **The Stranger** - Messenger or deceiver, savior or threat
          No. 3: **Language & Meaning** - Communication, symbol, and sign
          No. 4: **Eros** - Human sexuality and the life of the spirit

VOL. 21   No. 1: **Prophets & Prophecy** - Seeing beyond the veil
          No. 2: **The Soul** - Life within and beyond our corporeal existence
          No. 3: **Peace** - Seeking inner and outer tranquility
          No. 4: **Play & Work** - Struggle and relaxation in the search for meaning

VOL. 22   No. 1: **Ways of Knowing** - Different avenues to truth
          No. 2: **The Shadow** - Cast by the light we follow
          No. 3: **Conscience & Consciousness** - Inner guides to understanding one's being
          No. 4: **Miracles** - Enigmatic breaks in the laws of nature

VOL. 23   No. 1: **Millennium** - To what end, to what beginning?
          No. 2: **Ecstasy** - Joy that transports us outside of ourselves
          No. 3: **Fear** - Sign of weakness, or of strength?
          No. 4: **Birth and Rebirth** - The journey toward renewal

VOL. 24   No. 1: **Nature** - Exploring inner and outer terrain
          No. 2: **Prayer & Meditation** - Petition, praise, thanksgiving, confession
          No. 3: **Number & Symbol** - Languages that disclose the real
          No. 4: **Evil** - The duality within us, within the world

VOL. 25   No. 1: **Threshold** - Neither here nor there, neither real nor imaginary
          No. 2: **Riddle & Mystery** - Questions with answers, questions without answers
          No. 3: **The Teacher** - One who shows the way
          No. 4: **Fate and Fortune** - Inevitabilities that speak to us

VOL. 26   No. 1: **The Garden** - Cultivating within and without
          No. 2: **Light** - The brilliance of inner and outer illumination
          No. 3: **The Fool** - In search of divine innocence
          No. 4: **The Heart** - Where the Quest begins and ends

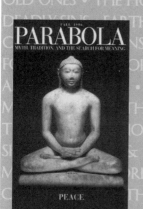
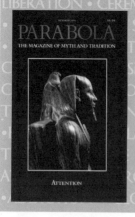
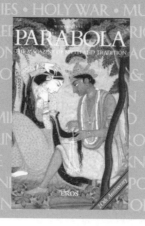